The Postmodern Explained

The Postmodern Explained

Correspondence 1982-1985

Jean-François Lyotard

Translation edited by Julian Pefanis and Morgan Thomas

Translations by Don Barry, Bernadette Maher, Julian Pefanis,
Virginia Spate, and Morgan Thomas

Afterword by Wlad Godzich

University of Minnesota Press
Minneapolis   London

Published by the University of Minnesota Press
2037 University Avenue Southeast, Minneapolis, MN 55414
Printed in the United States of America on acid-free paper

Library of Congress Cataloging-in-Publication Data

Lyotard, Jean-François.
    [Postmoderne expliqué aux enfants. English]
        The postmodern explained : correspondence, 1982–1985 / Jean-
    François Lyotard ; translation edited by Julian Pefanis and Morgan
    Thomas ; translations by Don Barry . . . [et al.] ; afterword by Wlad
    Godzich. — N. American ed.
      p.   cm.
    Translation of: Le Postmoderne expliqué aux enfants.
    Includes bibliographical references and index.
    ISBN 0-8166-2210-8 (hc). — ISBN 0-8166-2211-6 (pb)
    1. Postmodernism. 2. Lyotard, Jean-François — Correspondence.
  3. Philosophers — France — Correspondence.   I. Title.
B831.2L9513   1993
194 — dc20   92-10408
                                                 CIP

Contents

Preface to the French Edition

We have collected some letters by the author that take up the issue of postmodernity. Obtaining his consent to their publication was not without its difficulties. We argued that it could help to clear him of certain accusations: irrationalism, neoconservatism, intellectual terrorism, simple-minded liberalism, nihilism, and cynicism, among others. He seemed quite untroubled by these attributions. He said he saw them as a sign that, instead of reading (or what should be considered reading) and arguing *ad rem,* his opponents preferred to operate *ad hominem* and by ready-made categories. He said that it would not be paying thought its due respect to take any part in polemics of that kind.

But his main objection was the naïveté of these texts addressed to children; that, if they were published, their deceptive, pedagogical clarity would do nothing to lift the quality of a controversy that was already confused enough.

And, he added, he was too far from being clear about the question himself to venture a pronouncement on a hazy intuition.

But we believe (and this was the argument that caused him to relent) that it would not be a bad thing for even a vague sentiment (since signs of history are all it can offer as proof) — the presentiment that something is changing in our sensibilities — to appear unaffectedly and in all its indeterminacy. Far from being opposed to reason and probity, this incompletion, this childishness, respects in its own fashion the object of its Idea — contemporary history. And it is only as children that we can approach an understanding of this Idea.

We have taken out of this correspondence the passages that were not relevant to its main concerns. And we have left in repetitions from one letter to another. We are responsible for the preparation of the collection.

The Editors
Paris, December 25, 1985

Translator's Foreword

"What would happen if thought no longer had a child-hood?" In these pages Lyotard approaches the postmodern as a way of maintaining the possibility of thought "happening" — in philosophy, art, literature, and politics; of thought proceeding when it has lost faith in its capacity to repair the crimes of the past by guiding the present toward the end of the realization of ideas. If it is no longer possible, or credible, to assume the authority to speak for the future, what escape is there from an endless repetition of the already-said? But thought has to proceed.

Lyotard argues that it must do so by casting itself adrift from the chronophobia of the will, which sets out to plot or master the course of time — by allowing itself to be thrown off course. It has to relinquish its presumption, set out without knowing its destination or its destiny, leave itself open to the unfamiliarity of whatever may occur to it, and make rules in the absence of rules. The postmodern text will be in advance of itself: it will be writing written in the *what will have been* of the future anterior. It will be both premature (without presumption) and patient (awaiting the event of thought).

So the promise of the French title to "explain to children" what adults find obscure is surely ironic and not to be taken literally. It will not have explained the postmodern. Rather, it will have shown why it is necessary to approach the philosophical questions raised by postmodernity with patience and with the mind of the child. For childhood is the season of the mind's possibilities and of the possibility of philosophy. Lyotard points to something like the specific prematurity of the work of the postmodern artist and philosopher, the way its creation can occur too soon for its author, its conception too late. But if you read the letters on universal history and legitimation and consider that authority in the Soviet empire has today declared its position empty and its power void, you will see that a discussion about the collapse of the horizon of universal Ideals has never been more relevant.

We would like to thank the other "kids" who have helped us along the way with the translation of this book: Jelena Stojanovíc for her expert advice and Alan Cholodenko for his careful reading.

Sydney
December 25, 1991

Chapter 1

Answer to the Question, What Is the Postmodern?

To Thomas E. Carroll
Milan, May 15, 1982

A Demand

We are in a moment of relaxation — I am speaking of the tenor of the times. Everywhere we are being urged to give up experimentation, in the arts and elsewhere. I have read an art historian who preaches realism and agitates for the advent of a new subjectivity. I have read an art critic who broadcasts and sells "transavantgardism" in the marketplace of art. I have read that in the name of postmodernism architects are ridding themselves of the Bauhaus project, throwing out the baby — which is still experimentation — with the bathwater of functionalism. I have read that a new philosopher has invented something he quaintly calls Judeo-

Christianism, with which he intends to put an end to the current impiety for which we are supposedly responsible. I have read in a French weekly that people are unhappy with *A Thousand Plateaus* [by Deleuze and Guattari] because, especially in a book of philosophy, they expect to be rewarded with a bit of sense. I have read from the pen of an eminent historian that avant-garde writers and thinkers of the 1960s and 1970s introduced a reign of terror into the use of language, and that the imposition of a common mode of speech on intellectuals (that of historians) is necessary to reestablish the conditions for fruitful debate. I have read a young Belgian philosopher of language complaining that Continental thought, when faced with the challenge of talking machines, left them to look after reality; that it replaced the paradigm of referentiality with one of adlinguisticity (speaking about speech, writing about writing, intertextuality). He thinks it is time language recovered a firm anchoring in the referent. I have read a talented theatrologist who says the tricks and caprices of postmodernism count for little next to authority, especially when a mood of anxiety encourages that authority to adopt a politics of totalitarian vigilance in the face of the threat of nuclear war.

I have read a reputable thinker who defends modernity against those he calls neoconservatives. Under the banner of postmodernism they would like, he believes, to extricate themselves from the still-incomplete project of modernity, the project of Enlightenment. By his account, even the last partisans of the *Aufklärung* (the Enlightenment), for example, Popper and Adorno, were able to defend that project only in particular spheres of life — politics for the author of *The Open Society*, art for the author of *Aesthetic Theory*. Jürgen Habermas (you will have recognized him) thinks that if modernity has foundered, it is because the totality of life has been left to fragment into independent specialties given over to the narrow competence of experts, while concrete individual experiences "desublimated meaning" and "destructured form," not as a liberation, but in the manner of that immense ennui Baudelaire described over a century ago.

Following Albrecht Wellmer's lead, the philosopher believes the remedy for this parceling of culture and its separation from life will only come from a "change in the status of aesthetic experience when it is no longer primarily expressed in judgments of taste," when instead "it is used to illuminate a life-historical situation" — that is to say, when "it is related to the problems of existence." For this experience "then enters into a language game which is no longer just that of the aesthetic critic"; it intervenes "in cognitive procedures and normative expectations"; it "changes the way these different moments *refer* to one another." In short, Habermas demands of the arts and the experience they provide that they form a bridge over the gap separating the discourses of knowledge, ethics, and politics, thus opening the way for a unity of experience.

My problem is to be positive about what sort of unity Habermas has in mind. What is the end envisaged by the project of modernity? Is it the constitution of a sociocultural unity at the heart of which all elements of daily life and thought would have a place, as though within an organic whole? Or is the path to be cut between heterogeneous language games — knowledge, ethics, and politics — of a different order to them? And if so, how would it be capable of realizing their effective synthesis?

The first hypothesis, Hegelian in inspiration, does not call into question the notion of a dialectically totalizing *experience*. The second is closer in spirit to the *Critique of Judgment*, but like the *Critique* it must be submitted to the severe reexamination postmodernity addresses to the thought of the Enlightenment, to the idea of a uniform end of history and the idea of the subject. This critique was started not only by Wittgenstein and Adorno, but also by other thinkers, French or otherwise, who have not had the honor of being read by Professor Habermas. At least this spares them getting bad marks for neoconservatism.

Realism

The demands I cited to you at the beginning are not all equivalent. They may even be contradictory. Some are made in the name of postmodernism, some in opposition to it. It is not necessarily the same thing to demand the provision of a referent (and objective reality), or a meaning (and credible transcendence), or an addressee (and a public), or an addressor (and expressive subjectivity), or a communicative consensus (and a general code of exchange, the genre of historical discourse, for example). But in these various invitations to suspend artistic experimentation, there is the same call to order, a desire for unity, identity, security, and popularity (in the sense of *Öffentlichkeit*, "finding a public"). Artists and writers must be made to return to the fold of the community; or at least, if the community is deemed to be ailing, they must be given the responsibility of healing it.

There exists an irrefutable sign of this common disposition: for all these authors, nothing is as urgent as liquidating the legacy of the avant-gardes. The impatience of so-called transavantgardism is a case in point. The replies an Italian critic recently gave to French critics leave no doubt on the matter. The procedure of mixing avant-gardes together means that artists and critics can feel more confident of suppressing them than if they attacked them head-on. They can then pass off the most cynical eclecticism as an advance on the no doubt partial nature of earlier explorations. If they turned their backs on such explorations overtly, they would expose themselves to ridicule for neoacademicism. At the time the bourgeoisie was establishing itself in history, the salons and academies assumed a purgative function, awarding prizes for good conduct in the plastic and literary arts under the guise of realism. But capitalism in itself has such a capacity to derealize familiar objects, social roles, and institutions that so-called realist representations can no longer evoke reality except through nostalgia or derision — as an occasion for suffering rather than satisfaction. Classicism seems out of the question in a world where reality is so destabilized that it has no material to offer to experience, but only to analysis and experimentation.

This theme is familiar to readers of Walter Benjamin. Still, its precise implications need to be grasped. Photography did not pose an external challenge to painting any more than did industrial cinema to narrative literature. The former refined certain aspects of the program of ordering the visible elaborated by the Quattrocento, and the latter was able to perfect the containment of diachronies within organic totalities — the ideal of exemplary educative novels since the eighteenth century. The substitution of mechanical and industrial production for manual and craft production was not a catastrophe in itself, unless the essence of art is thought to be the expression of individual genius aided by the skills of an artisanal elite.

The greatest challenge lay in the fact that photographic and cinematic processes could accomplish better and faster — and with a diffusion a hundred thousand times greater than was possible for pictorial and narrative realism — the task that academicism had assigned to realism: protecting consciousness from doubt. Industrial photography and cinema always have the edge over painting and the novel when it is a matter of stabilizing the referent, of ordering it from a point of view that would give it recognizable meaning, of repeating a syntax and lexicon that would allow addressees to decode images and sequences rapidly, and make it easy for them to become conscious both of their own identities and of the approval they thereby receive from others — since the structures in these images and sequences form a code of communication among them all. So effects of reality — or the phantasms of realism, if you prefer — are multiplied.

If the painter and novelist do not want to be, in their turn, apologists for what exists (and minor ones at that), they must renounce such therapeutic occupations. They must question the rules of the art of painting and narration as learned and received from their predecessors. They soon find that such rules are so many methods of deception, seduction, and reassurance that make it impossible to be "truthful." An unprecedented split occurs in both painting and literature. Those who refuse to reexamine the rules of art will make careers in mass conformism, using "correct rules" to bring the endemic desire for reality into communication with objects and situations capable of satisfying it. Pornography is the use of photographs and film to this end. It becomes a general model for those pictorial and narrative arts that have not risen to the challenge of the mass media.

As for artists and writers who agree to question the rules of the plastic and narrative arts and perhaps share their suspicions by distributing their work — they are destined to lack credibility in the eyes of the devoted adherents of reality and identity, to find themselves without a guaranteed audience. In this sense, we can impute the dialectic of the avant-gardes to the challenge posed by the realisms of industry and the mass media to the arts of painting and literature. The Duchampian readymade does no more than signify, actively and parodically, this continual process of the dispossession of the painter's craft, and even the artist's. As Thierry de Duve astutely observes, the question of modern aesthetics is not "What is beautiful?" but "What is art to be (and what is literature to be)?"

Realism — which can be defined only by its intention of avoiding the question of reality implied in the question of art — always finds itself somewhere between academicism and kitsch. When authority takes the name of the party, realism and its complement, neoclassicism, triumph over the experimental avant-garde by slandering and censoring it. Even then, "correct" images, "correct" narratives — the correct forms that the party solicits, selects, and distributes — must procure a public that will desire them as the appropriate medicine for the depression and anxiety it feels. The demand for reality (that is, for unity, simplicity, communicability, etc.) did not have the same intensity or continuity for the German public between the wars as it had for the Russian public after the revolution: here one can draw a distinction between Nazi and Stalinist realism.

All the same, any attack on artistic experimentation mounted by political authority is inherently reactionary: aesthetic judgment would only have to reach a verdict on whether a particular work conforms to the established rules of the beautiful. Instead of the work's having to bother with what makes it an art object and whether it will find an appreciative audience, political academicism understands and imposes a priori criteria of the "beautiful," criteria that can, in one move and once and for all, select works and their public. So the use of categories in an aesthetic judgment would be similar to their use in a cognitive judgment. In Kant's terms, both would be determinant judgments: an expression is first "well formed" in the understanding; then, only those "cases" that can be subsumed within this expression are retained in experience.

When authority does not take the name of the party but that of capital, the "transavantgardist" solution (postmodernist in [Christopher] Jencks's sense) turns out to be more appropriate than the antimodern one. Eclecticism is the degree zero of contemporary general culture: you listen to reggae; you watch a western; you eat McDonald's at midday and local cuisine at night; you wear Paris perfume in Tokyo and dress retro in Hong Kong; knowledge is the stuff of TV game shows. It is easy to find a public for eclectic works. When art makes itself kitsch, it panders to the disorder that reigns in the "taste" of the patron. Together, artist, gallery owner, critic, and public indulge one another in the Anything Goes — it's time to relax. But this realism of Anything Goes is the realism of money: in the absence of aesthetic criteria it is still possible and useful to measure the value of works of art by the profits they realize. This realism accommodates every tendency just as capitalism accommodates every "need" — so long as these tendencies and needs have buying power. As for taste, there is no need to be choosy when you are speculating or amusing yourself. Artistic and literary investigation is doubly threatened: by "cultural politics" on one side, by the art and book market on the other. The advice it receives, from one or another of these channels, is to provide works of art that, first, relate to subjects already existing in the eyes of the public to whom they are addressed and, second, are made ("well formed") in such a way that this public will recognize what they are about, understand what they mean, and then be able to grant or withhold its approval with confidence, possibly even drawing some solace from those it accepts.

The Sublime and the Avant-Garde

This interpretation of the contact of the mechanical and industrial arts with the fine arts and literature is acceptable as an outline, but you would have to agree it is narrowly sociologistic and historicizing — in other words, one-sided. Notwithstanding the reservations of Benjamin and Adorno, it should be remembered that science and industry are just as open to suspicion with regard to reality as art and writing. To think otherwise would be to subscribe to an excessively humanist idea of the Mephistophelian functionalism of science and technology. One cannot deny the predominance of technoscience as it exists today, that is, the massive subordination of cognitive statements to the finality of the best possible performance — which is a technical criterion. Yet the mechanical and the industrial, particularly when they enter fields traditionally reserved for the artist, are bearers of something more than the effects of power. The objects and thoughts issuing from scientific knowledge and the capitalist economy bring with them one of the rules underwriting their possibility: the rule that there is no reality unless it is confirmed by a consensus between partners on questions of knowledge and commitment.

This rule is of no small consequence. It is the stamp left on the politics of both the scientist and the manager of capital by a sort of escape of reality from the metaphysical, religious, and political assurances the mind once believed it possessed. This retreat is indispensable to the birth of science and capitalism. There would be no physics had doubt not been cast on the Aristotelian theory of movement; no industry without the refutation of corporatism, mercantilism, and physiocracy. Modernity, whenever it appears, does not occur without a shattering of belief, without a discovery of the *lack of reality* in reality — a discovery linked to the invention of other realities.

What would this "lack of reality" mean if we were to free it from a purely historicizing interpretation? The phrase is clearly related to what Nietzsche calls nihilism. Yet I see a modulation of it well before Nietzschean perspectivism, in the Kantian theme of the sublime. In particular, I think the aesthetic of the sublime is where modern art (including literature) finds its impetus, and where the logic of the avant-garde finds its axioms.

The sublime feeling, which is also the feeling of the sublime, is, according to Kant, a powerful and equivocal emotion: it brings both pleasure and pain. Or rather, in it pleasure proceeds from pain. In the tradition of the philosophy of the subject coming from Augustine and Descartes — which Kant does not radically question — this contradiction (which others might call neurosis or masochism) develops as a conflict between all of the faculties of the subject, between the faculty to conceive of something and the faculty to "present" something. There is knowledge, first, if a statement is intelligible and, second, if "cases" that "correspond" to it can be drawn from experience. There is beauty if a particular "case" (a work of art), given first by the sensibility and with no conceptual determination, arouses a feeling of pleasure that is independent of any interest and appeals to a principle of universal consensus (which may never be realized).

Taste in this way demonstrates that an accord between the capacity to conceive and the capacity to present an object corresponding to the concept — an accord that is undetermined and without rule, giving rise to what Kant calls a reflective judgment — may be felt in the form of pleasure. The sublime is a different feeling. It occurs when the imagination in fact fails to present any object that could accord with a concept, even if only in principle. We have the Idea of the world (the totality of what is), but not the capacity to show an example of it. We have the Idea of the simple (the nondecomposable), but we cannot illustrate it by a sensible object that would be a case of it. We can conceive of the absolutely great, the absolutely powerful, but any presentation of an object — which would be intended to "display" that absolute greatness or absolute power — appears sadly lacking to us. These Ideas, for which there is no possible presentation and which therefore provide no knowledge of reality (experience), also prohibit the free accord of the faculties that produces the feeling of the beautiful. They obstruct the formation and stabilization of taste. One could call them unpresentable.

I shall call modern the art that devotes its "trivial technique," as Diderot called it, to presenting the existence of something unpresentable. Showing that there is something we can conceive of which we can neither see nor show — this is the stake of modern painting. But how do we show something that cannot be seen? Kant himself suggests the direction to follow when he calls *formlessness*, the *absence of form*, a possible index to the unpresentable. And, speaking of the empty *abstraction* felt by the imagination as it searches for a presentation of the infinite (another unpresentable), he says that it is itself like a presentation of the infinite, its *negative presentation*. He cites the passage "Thou shalt not make unto Thee any graven image, . . . " (Exodus 20:4) as the most sublime in the Bible, in that it forbids any presentation of the absolute. For an outline of an aesthetic of sublime painting, there is little we need to add to these remarks: as painting, it will evidently "present" something, but negatively. It will therefore avoid figuration or representation; it will be "blank" [*blanche*] like one of Malevich's squares; it will make one see only by prohibiting one from seeing; it will give pleasure only by giving pain. In these formulations we can recognize the axioms of the avant-gardes in painting, to the extent that they dedicate themselves to allusions to the unpresentable through visible presentations. The systems of reasoning in whose name or with which this task could support and justify itself warrant a good deal of attention; but such systems cannot take shape except by setting out from the vocation of the sublime, with the aim of legitimating this vocation — in other words, of disguising it. They remain inexplicable without the incommensurability between reality and concept implied by the Kantian philosophy of the sublime.

I do not intend to analyze in detail here the way the various avant-gardes have, as it were, humiliated and disqualified reality by their scrutiny of the pictorial techniques used to instill a belief in it. Local tone, drawing, the blending of colors, linear perspective, the nature of the support and of tools, "execution," the hanging of the work, the museum: the avant-gardes continually expose the artifices of presentation that allow thought to be enslaved by the gaze and diverted from the unpresentable. If Habermas, like Marcuse, takes this work of derealization as an aspect of the (repressive) "desublimation" characterizing the avant-garde, it is because he confuses the Kantian sublime with Freudian sublimation, and because for him aesthetics is still an aesthetics of the beautiful.

The Postmodern

What then is the postmodern? What place, if any, does it occupy in that vertiginous work of questioning the rules that govern images and narratives? It is undoubtedly part of the modern. Everything that is received must be suspected, even if it is only a day old ("Modo, modo," wrote Petronius). What space does Cézanne challenge? The Impressionists'. What object do Picasso and Braque challenge? Cézanne's. What presupposition does Duchamp break with in 1912? The idea that one has to make a painting — even a cubist painting. And [Daniel] Buren examines another presupposition that he believes emerged intact from Duchamp's work: the place of the work's presentation. The "generations" flash by at an astonishing rate. A work can become modern only if it is first postmodern. Thus understood, postmodernism is not modernism at its end, but in a nascent state, and this state is recurrent.

I would not wish, however, to be held to this somewhat mechanistic use of the word. If it is true that modernity unfolds in the retreat of the real and according to the sublime relationship of the presentable with the conceivable, we can (to use a musical idiom) distinguish two essential modes in this relationship. The accent can fall on the inadequacy of the faculty of presentation, on the nostalgia for presence experienced by the human subject and the obscure and futile will that animates it in spite of everything. Or else the accent can fall on the power of the faculty to conceive, on what one might call its "inhumanity" (a quality Apollinaire insists on in modern artists), since it is of no concern to the understanding whether or not the human sensibility or imagination accords with what it conceives — and on the extension of being and jubilation that come from inventing new rules of the game, whether pictorial, artistic, or something else. A caricatured arrangement of several names on the chessboard of avant-gardist history will show you what I mean: on the side of *melancholy,* the German Expressionists, on the side of *novatio,* Braque and Picasso; on the one hand, Malevich, on the other, El Lissitsky; on one side, De Chirico, on the other, Duchamp. What distinguishes these two modes may only be the merest nuance: they often coexist almost indiscernibly in the same piece, and yet they attest to a *différend* [a difference of opinion] within which the fate of thought has, for a long time, been played out, and will continue to be played out — a differend between regret and experimentation.

The works of Proust and Joyce both allude to something that does not let itself be made present. Allusion (to which

Paolo Fabbri has recently drawn my attention) is perhaps an indispensable mode of expression for works that belong to the aesthetic of the sublime. In Proust the thing that is eluded as the price of this allusion is the identity of consciousness, falling prey to an excess of time. But in Joyce it is the identity of writing that falls prey to an excess of the book, or literature. Proust invokes the unpresentable by means of a language that keeps its syntax and lexicon intact, and a writing that, in terms of most of its operators, is still part of the genre of the narrative novel. The literary institution as Proust inherits it from Balzac or Flaubert is undoubtedly subverted, since the hero is not a character but the inner consciousness of time, and also because the diachrony of the diegesis, already shaken by Flaubert, is further challenged by the choice of narrative voice. But the unity of the book as the odyssey of this consciousness is not disturbed, even if it is put off from chapter to chapter: the identity of the writing with itself within the labyrinth of its interminable narration is enough to connote this unity, which some have compared to that of *The Phenomenology of Spirit*. Joyce makes us discern the unpresentable in the writing itself, in the signifier. A whole range of accepted narrative and even stylistic operators is brought into play with no concern for the unity of the whole, and experiments are conducted with new operators. The grammar and vocabulary of literary language are no longer taken for granted; instead they appear as academicisms, rituals born of a piety (as Nietzsche might call it) that does not alter the invocation of the unpresentable.

So this is the differend: the modern aesthetic is an aesthetic of the sublime. But it is nostalgic; it allows the unpresentable to be invoked only as absent content, while form, thanks to its recognizable consistency, continues to offer the reader or spectator material for consolation and pleasure.

But such feelings do not amount to the true sublime feeling, which is intrinsically a combination of pleasure and pain: pleasure in reason exceeding all presentation, pain in the imagination or sensibility proving inadequate to the concept.

The postmodern would be that which in the modern invokes the unpresentable in presentation itself, that which refuses the consolation of correct forms, refuses the consensus of taste permitting a common experience of nostalgia for the impossible, and inquires into new presentations — not to take pleasure in them, but to better produce the feeling that there is something unpresentable. The postmodern artist or writer is in the position of a philosopher: the text he writes or the work he creates is not in principle governed by preestablished rules and cannot be judged according to a determinant judgment, by the application of given categories to this text or work. Such rules and categories are what the work or text is investigating. The artist and the writer therefore work without rules and in order to establish the rules for what *will have been made*. This is why the work and the text can take on the properties of an event; it is also why they would arrive too late for their author, or, in what amounts to the same thing, why the work of making them would always begin too soon. *Postmodern* would be understanding according to the paradox of the future (*post*) anterior (*modo*).

It seems to me that the essay (Montaigne) is postmodern, and the fragment (the *Athenaeum*) is modern.

Finally, it should be made clear that it is not up to us to *provide reality*, but to invent allusions to what is conceivable but not presentable. And this task should not lead us to expect the slightest reconciliation between "language games." Kant, in naming them the faculties, knew that they are separated by an abyss and that only a transcendental illusion (Hegel's) can hope to totalize them into a real unity. But he also knew that the price of this illusion is terror. The nineteenth and twentieth centuries have given us our fill of terror. We have paid dearly for our nostalgia for the all and the one, for a reconciliation of the concept and the sensible, for a transparent and communicable experience. Beneath the general demand for relaxation and appeasement, we hear murmurings of the desire to reinstitute terror and fulfill the phantasm of taking possession of reality. The answer is this: war on totality. Let us attest to the unpresentable; let us activate the differends and save the honor of the name.

Chapter 2

Apostil on Narratives

To Samuel Cassin
London, February 6, 1984

The more the discussion develops internationally, the more complex "the question of postmodernity" becomes. In 1979, I linked it to the problem of the "grand narratives" with the evident intention of simplifying it — but more than was necessary.

The "metanarratives" I was concerned with in *The Postmodern Condition* are those that have marked modernity: the progressive emancipation of reason and freedom, the progressive or catastrophic emancipation of labor (source of alienated value in capitalism), the enrichment of all humanity through the progress of capitalist technoscience, and even — if we include Christianity itself in modernity (in opposition to the classicism of antiquity) — the salvation of creatures through the conversion of souls to the Christian narrative of martyred love. Hegel's philosophy totalizes all of these narratives and, in this sense, is itself a distillation of speculative modernity.

These narratives are not myths in the sense that fables would be (not even the Christian narrative). Of course, like myths, they have the goal of legitimating social and political institutions and practices, laws, ethics, ways of thinking. Unlike myths, however, they look for legitimacy, not in an original founding act, but in a future to be accomplished, that is, in an Idea to be realized. This Idea (of freedom, "enlightenment," socialism, etc.) has legitimating value because it is universal. It guides every human reality. It gives modernity its characteristic mode: the *project*, the project Habermas says is still incomplete and must be resumed, renewed.

I would argue that the project of modernity (the realization of universality) has not been forsaken or forgotten but destroyed, "liquidated." There are several modes of destruction, several names that are symbols for them. "Auschwitz" can be taken as a paradigmatic name for the tragic "incompletion" of modernity.

But the victory of capitalist technoscience over the other candidates for the universal finality of human history is another means of destroying the project of modernity while giving the impression of completing it. The subject's mastery over the objects generated by contemporary science and technology does not bring greater freedom, more public education, or greater wealth more evenly distributed. It brings an increased reliance on facts.

Success is the only criterion of judgment technoscience will accept. Yet it is incapable of saying what success is, or why it is good, just, or true, since success is self-proclaiming,

like a ratification of something heedless of any law. It therefore does not complete the project of realizing universality
but in fact accelerates the process of delegitimation. This
is particularly what Kafka's work describes. And it is also
what the very principle of axiomatics signifies in scientific
formalizations.   .

Delegitimation is, of course, already part of modernity:
who can tell if Christ is the son of God or an impostor? His
Father forsook him. The martyrdom of Jesus finds a political
equivalent in the execution of the legitimate sovereign, Louis
XVI. What is the source of legitimacy in modern history
going to be after 1792? Supposedly the people. But the
people is an Idea — arguments and battles strive to establish
what the right Idea of the people is, and to make it prevail.
That is why there is a spread of civil war in the nineteenth
and twentieth centuries, and why even modern war between nations is always civil war: ''I,'' government of the
people, contest the legitimacy of *your* government. At
''Auschwitz,'' a modern sovereign, a whole people was
physically destroyed. The attempt was made to destroy it.
It is the crime opening postmodernity, a crime of *lèse-*
souveraineté [violated sovereignty] — not regicide this time,
but populicide (as distinct from ethnocide).

How could the grand narratives of legitimation still have
credibility in these circumstances?

This is not to suggest that there are no longer any credible narratives at all. By metanarratives or grand narratives,
I mean precisely narrations with a legitimating function.
Their decline does not stop countless other stories (minor
and not so minor) from continuing to weave the fabric of
everyday life.

In *The Postmodern Condition* and other books of that time
(at times in *Pagan Instructions*), I exaggerated the importance
to be given the narrative genre. It was a moment in a longer

and more radical inquiry, culminating in *The Differend*. Specifically, I went too far in identifying knowledge with narrative. It is not that theory is more objective than narrative: the historian's narrative is subject to roughly the same rules for establishing reality as the physicist's. But history as a narration has the added claim of being a science, not just fiction. Scientific theory, on the other hand, does not as a rule claim to be narrative (although contemporary astrophysics is happy to tell the story of the cosmos since the big bang). In other words, I think we now have to distinguish between different regimes of phrases and different genres of discourse. There is an uncriticized metaphysical element in general narratology that accords hegemony to one genre — the narrative — over all the others, a sort of sovereignty of minor narratives that allows them to escape the crisis of delegitimation. It is true that they escape, but only because they never had any legitimating value. The people's prose — the real prose, I mean — says one thing and its opposite: "Like father, like son" and "To the miserly father, a prodigal son." Only romanticism imagined this prose to be consistent, to be guided by the task of expressivity, emancipation, or the revelation of wisdom. Postmodernity is also the end of the people as sovereign of the stories.

One final remark about contemporary technoscience. It fulfills the project of modernity: man makes himself master and possessor of nature. But at the same time contemporary technoscience profoundly destabilizes that project. For the term "nature" must also include everything constituting the human subject: its nervous system, genetic code, cortical processor, visual and auditory receptors, communication systems (particularly linguistic), its organizations of group life, and so on. Its science and technoscience also end up being part of nature. There can be a science of science —

and there is — just as there is a science of nature. The same goes for technology: the whole field of STS (science-technology-society) appeared within a decade of the discovery of the subject's immanence in the object it studies and transforms. And vice versa: objects have languages; to know objects you must be able to translate their languages. Intelligence is therefore immanent in things. In these circumstances of the imbrication of subject and object, how could the ideal of mastery persist? It gradually falls out of use in the representations of science made by scientists themselves. Man is perhaps only a very sophisticated node in the general interaction of emanations constituting the universe.

Chapter 3

Missive on Universal History

To Mathias Kahn
Baltimore, November 15, 1984

It is inadvisable to grant the narrative genre an absolute privilege over other genres of discourse in the analysis of human, and specifically linguistic (ideological), phenomena, particularly when the approach is philosophical. Some of my earlier reflections may have succumbed to this "transcendental appearance" ("Presentations," *Pagan Instructions*, even *The Postmodern Condition*). On the other hand, an examination of "histories" might help us to address one of the great questions presented by the historical world at the end of the twentieth century (or the beginning of the twenty-first century). For if we claim that this world is historical, we necessarily intend to treat it narratively.

The question that concerns me is this: can we today continue to organize the mass of events coming from the human
and nonhuman world by referring them to the Idea of a
universal history of humanity? I do not intend to deal with
this question philosophically here. Nonetheless its formulation calls for a number of clarifications.

I start out by asking, Can we *continue* to organize . . . ? The
word implies that previously we could organize these
things. And here I am in fact referring to a tradition: that
of modernity. Modernity is not an epoch but a mode (the
word's Latin origin) within thought, speech, and sensibility.
Erich Auerbach saw its emergence in the writing of Augustine's *Confessions:* the destruction of the syntactical architecture of classical discourse and the adoption of a paratactic
arrangement of short sentences linked by the most elemen-
tary of conjunctions: the *and.* Like Bakhtin, Auerbach also
encounters this mode in Rabelais, then in Montaigne.

For my part, and without trying to justify this view here,
I see a sign of it in the genre of first-person narration chosen
by Descartes to explain his method. The *Discourse* is also
a confession. But what it confesses is not the dispossession
of the "I" by God, but the effort of the "I" to master every
given, including itself. Descartes tries to graft the finality
of a series directed toward the mastery and possession of
"nature" onto the contingency that the *and* leaves between
sequences conveyed by phrases. (Whether or not he suc-
ceeds is a different matter.) This modern mode of organizing time is further developed in the eighteenth century
in the *Aufklärung.*

The thought and action of the nineteenth and twentieth
centuries are governed by an Idea (in the Kantian sense):
the Idea of emancipation. It is, of course, framed in quite
different ways, depending on what we call the philosophies

of history, the grand narratives that attempt to organize this mass of events: the Christian narrative of the redemption of original sin through love; the *Aufklärer* narrative of emancipation from ignorance and servitude through knowledge and egalitarianism; the speculative narrative of the realization of the universal Idea through the dialectic of the concrete; the Marxist narrative of emancipation from exploitation and alienation through the socialization of work; and the capitalist narrative of emancipation from poverty through technoindustrial development. Between these narratives there are grounds for litigation and even for differends. But in all of them, the givens arising from events are situated in the course of a history whose end, even if it remains beyond reach, is called universal freedom, the fulfillment of all humanity.

Second clarification. When one says, "Can we continue to organize . . . ?" one at least assumes — even if the answer (intended or not) is negative (that we cannot) — the persistence of a *we* capable of thinking or experiencing that continuity or discontinuity. The question also asks, What constitutes this *we*? As the pronoun in the first-person plural indicates, it concerns a community of subjects, you and me, or them and me, depending on whether the speaker is addressing other members of the community (you/me) or a third party (you/them + me) for whom these other members — represented by the speaker — are designated by the third person (them). The question asks whether this *we* is or is not independent of the Idea of a history of humanity.

In the tradition of modernity, the movement of emancipation is one in which the third party, initially external to the *we* of the emancipatory avant-garde, will end up joining the community of speakers, whether actual (first person) or potential (second person). There will be only you and me.

In this tradition the place of the first person is in fact marked by the control of speech and meaning: let the people have a say in politics, let the worker have a say in society, let the poor have a say in economics, let the particular assume the universal, and let the last also become the first. Excuse me for simplifying.

It follows that, caught between the actual situation of minorities (where there are many third parties and not many of *you and me*) and the unanimity still to come (when every third person will be banished by definition), the *we* of my question exactly reproduces the tension humanity must experience in its vocation for emancipation, a tension between the particularity, randomness, and opacity of the present and the universality, self-determination, and transparency of the future promised by emancipation. If this tension is exactly the same, the *we* asking the question — "Shall we continue to think and act in the name of the Idea of a history of humanity?" — is also raising the question of its own identity as established by the tradition of modernity. And if the answer to the question should be no (no, human history is no longer credible as a universal history of emancipation), then the status of the *we* asking the question will also have to be revised.

The *we*, it seems, will be condemned (but a condemnation only in the eyes of modernity) to remain particular, to be you and me (perhaps), to leave many third parties on the outside. But, since this *we* has not forgotten (yet) that third parties were once potential and even promised first persons, it will have to resign itself to the loss of unanimity and find another mode of thought and action, or else sink into incurable melancholy for this lost "object" (or impossible subject): liberated humanity. In either case we are affected by a sort of grief. The work of mourning, according to Freud, involves recovering from the loss of a loved object by transferring the investment in the lost object to the subject — from them to us.

Still, there are other ways of dealing with it. One is secondary narcissism. According to many observers, it is now the dominant mode of thought and action in developed societies. I fear it may be no more than the blind (and compulsive) repetition of an earlier bereavement — the loss of God — which in truth gave rise to the mode of modernity and its project of conquest. Such a conquest today would do no more than perpetuate the conquests of the moderns, differing only in its renunciation of a search for unanimity. Terror would no longer be exercised for the sake of freedom but for "our" satisfaction, the satisfaction of a *we* permanently restricted to its particularity. Would it still be too modern if I were to find this perspective intolerable? The word for it is tyranny: the law "we" proclaim is not addressed to *you*, fellow citizens, or even subjects; it is applied to *them*, the third parties, those on the outside, without the least concern for legitimating it in their eyes. As I recall, this was Nazism's way of dealing with emancipation and its way of exercising a terror whose logic, for the first time in Europe since 1789, was not in principle accessible to all and whose benefits could not be shared by all.

A different way of dealing with the universal emancipation promised by modernity would be to "work over" (in the Freudian sense) not just the loss of this object but also the loss of the subject to whom this goal was promised. It would be a matter not only of recognizing our finitude, but of elaborating the status of the *we*, the question of the subject — that is, of escaping both an unrevised renewal of the modern subject and its parodical or cynical repetition (tyranny). Such elaboration, I believe, can only lead to an immediate abandonment of the linguistic structure of communication (I/you/he), which the moderns, whether consciously or not, held up as their ontological and political model.

My third clarification will concentrate on the words *Can we?* in the question, "Can we today continue to organize events according to the Idea of a universal history of humanity?" As understood by Aristotle and linguists, the modality of the *possible* [*pouvoir*] applied to a notion (here the pursuit of universal history) contains at once its affirmation and negation. That this pursuit is possible implies neither that it will take place nor that it will not take place, but that what certainly will take place is the fact that it will or will not take place. There is uncertainty about the contents, the dictum (the notion's affirmation or negation), but necessity regarding the subsequent fact, or *modus*. We recognize here Aristotle's thesis of contingent futures. (They still have to be dated.)

But the expression *Can we?* not only connotes possibility, it implies capacity as well: is it in our power, our strength, and our competence to perpetuate the project of modernity? The question suggests that to be sustained, such a project would call for strength and competence, and that these things may have failed us. Such a reading would have to spark an inquiry, an inquiry into the failing of the modern subject. And if this failing should be a matter for dispute, then we must be able to produce evidence for it in the form of facts or at least signs. The interpretation of this evidence may well engender controversy, and at the very least it must be submitted to cognitive procedures for establishing facts or speculative procedures for validating signs. (I am referring, without further explanation, to the Kantian problematic of hypotyposes that plays a major role in his historicopolitical philosophy.)

Without wishing to decide here and now whether it is constituted by facts or signs, the evidence we can collect on this failing of the modern subject seems difficult to refute. In the course of the past fifty years, each grand narrative of emancipation — regardless of the genre it privileges — has, as it were, had its principle invalidated. *All that is real is rational, all that is rational is real:* "Auschwitz" refutes the speculative doctrine. At least this crime, which is real, is not rational. *All that is proletarian is communist, all that is communist is proletarian:* "Berlin 1953," "Budapest 1956," "Czechoslovakia 1968," "Poland 1980" (to name but a few) refute the doctrine of historical materialism: the workers rise up against the Party. *All that is democratic is by the people and for the people, and vice versa:* "May 1968" refutes the doctrine of parliamentary liberalism. Everyday society brings the representative institution to a halt. *Everything that promotes the free flow of supply and demand is good for general prosperity, and vice versa:* the "crises of 1911 and 1929" refute the doctrine of economic liberalism, and the "crisis of 1974–79" refutes the post-Keynesian modification of that doctrine.

The investigator records the names of these events as so many signs of the failing of modernity. The grand narratives have become scarcely credible. One is then tempted to give credence to a grand narrative of the decline of the grand narratives. But as we know, the grand narrative of decadence was already in place at the beginning of Western thought, in Hesiod and Plato. It follows the narrative of emancipation like a shadow. So nothing would have changed — except that extra strength and competence will be needed to face the task at hand. Many believe this is the moment for religion, a moment to rebuild a credible narration where the wounds of this fin de siècle will be recounted, where they will be healed. They claim that myth is the originary genre; that in myth the thought of origin is present in its originary paradox; and that we must raise myth from the ruins to which it has been reduced by rational, demythologizing and positivistic thought.

But this course of action, it seems to me, is far from being just. Besides, we should note that in this brief description the expression *to be able* [*pouvoir*] has undergone a further modification, signaled in the way I have used the word *just*. To the question, Can we perpetuate the grand narratives? the answer has become: we *ought* to do this or that. *Being able* also implies having the right; in this sense, the expression draws thought into the universe of deontics: the slippage from right to duty is as easy as that from the permissible to the obligatory. The issue here is the contingency of the linkage to the situation that I have described as the failing of modernity. Many types of linkages are possible, and one has to decide. Deciding nothing is still deciding. Remaining silent is still speaking. Politics always rests on the way one phrase, the present phrase, is linked to another phrase. It is not about the volume of discourse or the importance of the speaker or addressee. From the different phrases that are actually possible, one will be actualized, and the actual question is, which one? The description of this failing does not give us any clue to the answer. This is why the word *postmodernity* is able to embrace such conflicting perspectives. These few remarks are simply meant to indicate the antimythologizing direction I think we should take in "working over" the loss of the modern *we*.

* * *

Now to the topic indicated by my title. I wonder if the failing of modernity — in the form of what Adorno described as the collapse of metaphysics (for him, concentrated in the failure of the affirmative dialectic of Hegelian thought in the face of the Kantian thesis of obligation or the event of senseless annihilation named Auschwitz) — could be connected to a resistance on the part of what I shall call the multiplicity of worlds of names, the insurmountable diversity of cultures. Taking this approach to the question in conclusion, I want to go back and reappraise several of the issues I noted earlier, regarding the universality of the grand narratives, the status of the *we*, the reason for the failing of modernity, and finally the contemporary issue of legitimation.

As child or immigrant, one enters a culture through an apprenticeship in proper names. One must learn the names that designate near relations, heroes (in a general sense), places, dates, and also, I would add (following Kripke), units of measure, space, time, and exchange value. These names are "rigid designators": they signify nothing or at least can be laden with various and conflicting significations; they can be attached to phrases belonging to altogether heterogeneous regimes (descriptive, interrogative, ostensive, evaluative, prescriptive, etc.) and included in incommensurable genres of discourse (cognitive, persuasive, epideictic, tragic, comic, dithyrambic, etc.). Names are not learned by themselves — they are lodged in little stories. Again, narrative's strength lies in its capacity to hold together a multiplicity of heterogeneous families of discourse — so it has to be "inflatable," if I may put it that way. Narrative arranges these families of discourse into a sequence of events determined by the culture's proper names.

The great coherence of this organization is reinforced by the narrative's mode of transmission, most visibly in what I shall call, for convenience, "savage" societies. André Marcel d'Ans writes: "Among the Cashinahua, every interpretation of a *miyoi* (myth, tale, legend, or traditional narrative) opens with a fixed formula: 'Here is the story of . . . as I have always heard it told. It is now my turn to tell it to you. Listen!' And the recitation invariably closes with another formula which goes: 'Here ends the story of . . . He who told it to you is . . . (Cashinahua name), known to the whites as . . . (Spanish or Portuguese name).' " The ethnologist tells us, the whites, how the Cashinahua storyteller tells the story of a Cashinahua hero to a Cashinahua audience. He can do this because he is himself a (male) Cashinahua listener — and he is a listener because he bears a Cashinahua name. So a ritual using strict denominations defines the narration's audience and recurrence. All the phrases contained in such narrations are, as it were, fastened to named or nameable instances in the world of Cashinahua names. The universe presented by any one of these phrases, regardless of its regime, refers to this world of names. The hero or heroes and places presented, the addressee, and lastly the addressor are all meticulously named.

To hear the narratives, you have to have been named. (All males and girls prior to puberty may listen.) The same applies to telling them (only men may). And to having your story told (to be the referent) as well (all the Cashinahua can, without exception). By putting names into stories, the narration keeps the rigid designators of its common identity sheltered from events of the "moment" and·the danger of what could be linked to it. To be named is to be narrated. There are two aspects to this: every narrative, even ones that seem anecdotal, reactualizes names and the relations between names. In reciting its narratives, the community reassures itself of the permanence and legitimacy of its world of names through the recurrence of this world in its stories. In addition, some narratives are explicitly stories of naming.

When we directly raise the question of the origin of tradition or authority among the Cashinahua, we come up against the usual paradox in such cases. If we suppose that a phrase cannot be authorized unless the addressor holds some authority, what happens when the addressor's authority results from the meaning of the phrase? The phrase, in legitimating the addressor presented by its universe, legitimates itself in the eyes of the addressee. The Cashinahua narrator draws the authority to tell stories from his name. But his name is authorized by his stories, particularly by stories that tell of the genesis of names. This *circulus vitiosus* is typical.

We see here the discursive procedures of what might be called "a very large scale integrated culture." Identification reigns absolutely. Being self-enclosed, it eliminates the debris of the narratives — unassimilable events — by making sacrifices, drug taking (in the case of the Cashinahua), or fighting border wars.

Mutatis mutandis, this is the mechanism of a culture's self-identification. Its disintegration in situations of servile dependency, colonial or imperialist, spells the destruction of cultural identity. But in struggles for independence, this mechanism becomes the guerrillas' major asset, since narrative and its transmission give the resistance an immediate legitimacy (or right) and logistics (means of transmitting messages, coordinates of sites and of times, use of knowledge about natural phenomena in the cultural tradition, etc.).

As I have said, legitimacy is secured by the strength of the narrative mechanism: it encompasses the multiplicity of families of phrases and possible genres of discourse; it envelops every name; it is always actualizable and always has been; both diachronic and parachronic, it secures mastery over time and therefore over life and death. Narrative is authority itself. It authorizes an infrangible *we*, outside of which there is only *they*.

This kind of organization is absolutely opposed to the organization of the grand narratives of legitimation that characterize modernity in the West. These narratives are cosmopolitical, as Kant would say. They involve precisely an "overcoming" [*dépassement*] of the particular cultural identity in favor of a universal civic identity. But how such an overcoming can take place is not apparent.

There is nothing in the savage community to lead it to transform itself dialectically into a society of citizens. Saying that it is "human" and that it already prefigures a universality is settling the issue in advance: having assumed a universal history, the humanist inscribes the particular community into it as a moment in the universal becoming of human communities. This is also, *grosso modo*, the axiom of the grand narrative of speculative thought applied to human history. But the question is whether there is a history of humanity. The epistemological account is the most cautious but also the most deceptive: anthropologists use the rules of the cognitive genre to describe the narrations of savage communities and their rules, without claiming to establish any continuity between the rules they are describing and the rules of their own mode of discourse. In the Lévi-Straussian account, anthropologists are able to introduce an identity of functioning, a so-called structural identity, between myth and the explanation of myth — but only at the expense of abandoning any attempt to find an intelligible passage between them. There can be identity, but no history.

All of these difficulties are well known — and trivial. I remind you of them only because they may make it easier to assess the extent of the present failing of modernity. It is as though the enormous effort, marked by the name of the Declaration of Rights, seeking to deprive peoples of their narrative legitimacy (shall we say lying upstream in the course of time) and make them take up the Idea of free citizenship (lying downstream) as the only legitimacy — it is as though that effort, which has taken so many different paths over the past two centuries, had failed. A premonitory sign of this failure might be seen in the very designation of the author of this declaration of universal import: "We, the French people."

The workers' movement is a particularly telling example of this failure. In theory, its internationalism meant that the legitimacy of the class struggle derived not from local (popular or labor) traditions but from an Idea to be realized — the Idea of the worker emancipated from the proletarian condition. Now we know that, from the time of the Franco-Prussian War of 1870–71, the International was deadlocked over the issue of Alsace-Lorraine, and that in 1914 both German and French Socialists voted for national war budgets. Stalinism as "socialism in one country," and the suppression of the Comintern, openly proclaimed the superiority of the nation's proper name over the universal name of the Soviets. The spread of struggles for independence since the Second World War and the recognition of new national names seem to imply a consolidation of local legitimacies and the vanishing of a universal horizon of emancipation. New "independent" governments either fall in line with the market of world capitalism or adopt a Stalinist-style political apparatus — "leftists" with their sights set on that horizon are eliminated without mercy. As the current slogan of the far right in France would have it: Put the French first (implying: leave freedoms until later).

You could argue that these retreats into local legitimacy are reactions of resistance to the devastating effects of imperialism, and its malaise, on particular cultures. That is true, and it confirms the diagnosis, or makes it even worse. There is no trace of a cosmopolitan perspective to be found in the way the world market reconstituted itself after the Second World War, or in the intense economic and financial battle now being conducted for domination of this market by multinational banks and companies — with the support of national states. Even supposing the parties to this game still prided themselves on achieving the goals set by economic liberalism, or by Keynesianism in the modern era, it would still be difficult to give them any credit on this score. Obviously their game, far from reducing the inequality of wealth in the world, exacerbates it, and far from breaking down barriers, exploits them for commercial and monetary speculation. The world market does not constitute universal history in the modern sense. Moreover, cultural differences are promoted at every opportunity in the guise of tourist and cultural commodities.

What, finally, is this *we* that tries to reflect on this predicament of failing, if it is no longer the core, minority, or avant-garde that anticipates today what liberated humanity might be tomorrow? By trying to reflect on this predicament, are we condemning ourselves to be no more than negative heroes? It is at least clear that a certain image of the intellectual (Voltaire, Zola, Sartre) is caught up with this failing. This was an image sustained by the acknowledged legitimacy of the Idea of emancipation, an image that shadowed the history of modernity through thick and thin. But the violence of the critique mounted against schooling in the 1960s, followed by the inexorable erosion of teaching institutions in every modern country, is enough to show that learning and its transmission no longer command the authority that once made us listen to intellectuals when they moved from the lectern to the podium. In a world where success means gaining time, thinking has a single, but irredeemable, fault: it is a waste of time.

That, in general terms, is the question I am posing — or rather the question I believe poses itself. I did not intend to answer it, just to discuss it. When we meet, we will be able to discuss more fully the aspects of its elaboration that

I have not considered in this missive. After the age of the intellectual, the age of the party, it would be interesting if, on each side of the Atlantic, without presumption, we could begin to trace a line of resistance to the failing of modernity.

Chapter 4

Memorandum on Legitimation

To Alexandre Demoule
New York, November 26, 1984

I would like to approach the question of totalitarianism from the apparently narrow perspective of the language of legitimation. I believe this is a more radical approach than any other (politicological, sociological, or historical) in that it does not appeal to received, often unquestioned, entities like power, society, the people, or tradition. Furthermore, it seems to me that such an approach can help us to distinguish between different states of totalitarianism, while the term, itself somewhat totalizing, tends to conceal or confuse them.

I will begin by reminding you of a distinction made by Kant (who thus attaches himself to the political philosophy of the critical Enlightenment) without explaining my decision to resort to it here. In *Perpetual Peace* (second section, first article), Kant distinguishes between the *forma imperii*, the form according to which supreme authority is exercised, and the form of government (*forma regiminis*), the principle according to which the state makes use of its power. The first of these, the form of sovereignty (*Beherrschung*), consists in the delegation of supreme power: either to a single person (autocracy) or to several people (aristocracy) or to everybody (democracy). The second, the form of government (*Regierung*), is either despotic or republican, depending on whether or not executive and legislative powers are combined. Kant is quick to add that the democratic form, that is, the mode of sovereignty that directly confers the exercise of public power upon all citizens without the mediation of representative instances, calls for a form of government that is necessarily despotic. This is because the people as sovereign is at the same time both legislator and executor of its own decisions. Conversely, according to Kant, an autocrat like Frederick II of Prussia can exercise his authority in a manner that is analogous to republicanism (in terms of government).

The question of legitimacy is not, as you know, treated directly in this passage from *Perpetual Peace*. I would like, however, to graft it onto the distinction between despotic and republican governments in the following way.

We could call the subject of the normative phrase its legitimating instance. A phrase is termed normative when it gives the force of law to its object, a prescriptive phrase. For the prescription *it is obligatory for x to perform action* a, the normative phrase would be *it is a norm decreed by y that it is obligatory for x to perform action* a. In this formulation the normative phrase designates, here in the name of *y*, the instance that legitimates the prescription addressed to x. The legislative power is held by y. The despotism and republicanism described by Kant can easily be located within this little complex of phrases.

If we now ask who y could be to command such legislative authority, we soon find ourselves slipping into the usual aporias. We encounter the vicious circle: y has authority over x because x authorizes y to have it; the *petitio principii*: the authorization authorizes the authority (i.e., it is the normative phrase that authorizes y to set the norm); the infinite regress: x is authorized by y, who is authorized by z, and so on; the paradox of the idiolect (in Wittgenstein's sense): God, Life, or any big A designates y to exercise authority, but y is the only witness to this revelation.

I would argue that, at least in the framework of a reflection on totalitarianism, there are two primary procedures of language that come to mask the logical aporia of authorization (or fill the ontological gap) that such a reflection would disclose. Both of these procedures make recourse to narration; that is, on the surface at least, they both disperse this absence, spreading the theoretical problem along the diachronic axis. But that is the only thing they have in common. For while one procedure directs this dispersion upstream, toward an origin, the other directs it downstream, toward an end. In very simple terms (which you will have to excuse), one of these narrations shapes those mythic narratives that are essential to traditional communities, while the other shapes the narratives of emancipation (which I called metanarratives in *The Postmodern Condition*).

At this point I would like to clarify their respective functions — without losing sight of the question of totalitarianism.

To be completely clear, I should really begin by setting out the questions of language that form the basis for my argument in this memorandum. I cannot do that here, so I will make do with a quick summary. Language is the object of an Idea. It is not like a box of tools that "speakers" (human, in general) dip into when they want to communicate or express themselves. If we free ourselves of this functionalist approach, we will notice that the only *givens* are phrases, in their hundreds and thousands. We see that these phrases do not simply convey meanings: however unassuming and ephemeral (or silent) they may be, they situate, within the universe they present, an addressor, an addressee, and a referent. We see that we can distinguish different families or regimes of phrases from one another, since it is impossible to convert one phrase into another without modifying what I will simply call the pragmatic situation of the instances I have just mentioned (referent, addressee, addressor). *The door is closed* is a descriptive phrase. In the universe it presents, the question is whether or not the door is closed: it is therefore governed by the criterion of truth or falsity. *Close the door* is a prescriptive phrase, and the question it raises hinges on the justice of the order given to the addressee and on the execution of the act it prescribes. As we can see, the regime governing a normative phrase is completely different from the regime governing a prescriptive phrase. The same is true of interrogative, performative (in the strict sense), and exclamatory phrases.

The other point underlying my argument, and one that I think is essential for an understanding of totalitarianism, is that each phrase, no matter how ordinary, arrives as an event. I am not saying that each phrase is exceptional, sensational, or unprecedented, but that what it contains is never necessary. It is necessary *that* something happens (the event), but *what* happens (the phrase, its meaning, object, interlocutors) is never necessary — the necessity of contingency or, if you like, the being of nonbeing. The linkage between phrase and phrase is not, as a rule, predetermined. Genres of discourse clearly exist: exposition (like the present one), the genre of dialectics (which we call discussion), the genre of comedy, the genre of tragedy, satire (the genre of genres), the essay, the diary, and so forth. These genres of discourse set rules for the linking of phrases to ensure that the discourse proceeds toward its generically assigned end: to convince, to persuade, to inspire laughter or tears, and so forth. Respecting these rules thus allows the linking of phrases toward a generic end. But, as you would know, these rules of linking are seldom (if ever) respected outside of classical poetics and rhetoric. Modern writers and artists continually break these rules, precisely because they set a greater value on questioning the event than on worrying about imitation or conformity. Like Auerbach, I would put Augustine among modern writers, next to Rabelais, Montaigne, Shakespeare, Sterne, Joyce, and Stein. What is interesting about these modern infractions is not that they are transgressive, as Bataille thought, but that they constantly open the question of nothingness, the question of the event. This is demonstrated by Benjamin with regard to Baudelaire, and by Barthes with his theory of the text and writing.

Let us now return to our reflection on the narrative of legitimation and totalitarianism. First, mythic narration.

The old question — is myth originary or origin mythic? — goes back to Schelling. Freud struggled with the same question. (Your mother has written an impressive study on this subject.) The corpus of narratives of a traditional ethnic group — the Cashinahua as studied by André Marcel d'Ans — together with its ritual of transmission, is composed of narratives of origin, myths in the strict sense, and also little stories, tales, and legends. The important thing for our question seems to me to be the pragmatics of narration itself rather than the analysis of narrative contents. To *hear* a Cashinahua narrative, one has to be an adult male or a girl prior to puberty, and one must have a Cashinahua name (as does the anthropologist). To *recount* a narrative, one has to be a man and have a Cashinahua name. Finally, every Cashinahua without exception can *form the object* of one of these narratives. In this sense, the transmission of narratives is subject to constraints. These constraints are used to effect the separation of the community into kinship groups governing exogamous unions: among the Cashinahua there are two masculine and two feminine "moieties," with two age groups in each moiety — eight kinship groups in all. And, as the ethnologist notes, "exogamous unions have the explicit function of transmitting *names.*" The constraints acting on the pragmatics of narration should be understood as rules for the authentication and conservation of narratives, and therefore of the community itself, through the repetition of names.

The ethnologist confirms this, noting that every narration opens with a set formula: "Here is the story of . . . as I've always heard it. I am, in turn, going to tell it to you. Listen!" He adds that the recitation invariably closes with another formula: "Here ends the story of . . . He who told it to you is . . . (Cashinahua name), known to the whites as . . . (Spanish or Portuguese name)." Each time the story is told, this narrative ritual fastens it to the names of the three instances (the narrator, his listener, and the hero) and thus legitimates the story by inscribing it in the world of Cashinahua names.

The effect of this is a process characteristic of historical time. Each narrator declares that he is telling the story as he has "always heard" it. He was a listener to this story and the narrator he heard it from was, in his turn, also once a listener. It is the same all the way along the chain of transmission. It follows that the heroes themselves must have been the first narrators. The time of the diegesis, when the action described takes place, and the time of the actual narration that decribes this action, communicate without interruption. Two operations ensure such a panchrony: the permanence of names (which are finite in number and bestowed on individuals by a system independent of time) and the permutability of named individuals across the three narrative instances (narrator, listener, hero), which is governed by ritual on each occasion.

I believe this apparatus of language exemplifies our first *forma regiminis,* the form of government, or regime, that Kant called despotism, and the legitimation of the normative instance corresponding to that form. Names, or what Kripke calls "rigid designators," define a world, a world of names — the cultural world. This world is finite because in it the number of available names is finite. This world has forever been the same. Each human comes into this world with a place, that is, with a name that will determine his or her relationship to other names. This place in effect controls the sexual, economic, social, and linguistic exchanges that one has the right or the duty to have (or not to have) with others who bear names. An event (there we are) can only be introduced into the tradition when it is framed within a story — a story subject to the rules of naming as much in what it tells (its referents: heroes, places, times) as in the manner of its telling (its narrator, its audience). So the void that in principle separates two phrases, and makes the phrase into an event, is filled by narrative, itself subordinate to the repetition of the world of names and to the permutation of names across the instances. In this way the Cashinahua identity, the *we* that draws together the three narrative instances, escapes the vertigo of contingency and nothingness. And as narrative has an intrinsic capacity to collect, arrange, and transmit descriptions, as well as prescriptions, evaluations, and feelings (exclamatory and interrogative phrases, for example), this tradition transmits obligations attached to names, along with prescriptions for particular situations, and legitimates them simply by placing them under the authority of the Cashinahua name.

The Cashinahua call themselves "the true men." Whatever stands outside this tradition — any event, natural or human, for which there is no name — is *not*, for it is not authorized (not "true"). Authority is not *represented* in the modern sense of the term: the Cashinahua people legislate through the transmission of their narratives and, in performing them (since names create all sorts of obligations), exercise executive power. So there is certainly a kind of politics at play in this narrative practice, but it is immersed in the totality of life instituted by the narratives and could, in this sense, be said to be "totalitarian."

I am conscious that my description is somewhat simplistic. An ethnologist would have little trouble refuting my conclusions — by showing how my analysis flows from the ancient desire of the West to discover in the exotic the figure of what it has lost, as Plato did long ago in Egypt and Atlantis. I completely agree with this criticism. Our vision of myth is itself probably mythic; what we do with Cashinahua stories is evidently far less amusing than what the Cashinahua do themselves. Yet for the problematic that concerns us here, modern totalitarianism, this tendency to exaggerate the value of narrative as archaic legitimation is interesting in itself. It is even essential.

This overvaluation, still prevalent in attitudes and still potentially active, may explain why Nazism could be successful in resorting to myth when it pitted its own despotic authority against the republican authority that defined modern political life in the West, initially against the Weimar. Nazism put the Aryan name in the place occupied by the Idea of the citizen. Abandoning the modern horizon of cosmopolitanism, it grounded its legitimacy in the saga of the Nordic peoples. The reason it could succeed was that it released in the sovereign people, "democratically" in Kant's sense, a desire to "return to the source," a desire only mythology could satisfy. Nazism provided the people with names and narratives that permitted them to identify exclusively with Germanic heroes and heal the wounds inflicted by the event of defeat and crisis. Xenophobia and chronophobia are necessarily implicated in this use of language as an apparatus of legitimation. I will come back to this.

Republicanism is more than the separation of powers: it demands the fission, even the disintegration, of popular identity. It is not just about representation: from the perspective of language, it is an organization of regimes of phrases and genres of discourse that relies on their dissociation, thus allowing a "play" between them or, if you prefer, preserving the possibility of accounting for the event in its contingency. This organization I will call *deliberative*.

As we have seen, in traditional narration the combination of multiple stakes — converting, informing, convincing, persuading, and so on — is concealed by the homogeneity of the story's unfolding. The organic and (I would say) totalizing character of narrative does not lend itself to analysis. On the other hand, it is easy to dismantle the arrangement of genres of discourse and regimes of phrases in deliberative politics. A simple, even naive description of the moments of the deliberative process will make this easy to understand:

1. The highest end is formulated in a canonical phrase (let's call it the stake) that is an interrogative prescriptive: *What ought we to be?* The phrase is full of possible meanings: *happy, wise, free, equal, rich, powerful, artistic, American?* The answers are examined in the philosophies of history; in the political arena they are scarcely discussed, though they are present in the phrase "kindred spirits."

2. To the *What ought we to be?* is linked a *What ought we to do in order to be that?* In this way, one moves from a pure, almost ethical prescription to a hypothetical imperative, such as: If you want to be this, then do that.

3. The previous question calls for an inventory of the means to attain this end: an analysis of the situation, a description of the resources available to both allies and adversaries, and a definition of their respective interests. This is a completely different genre of discourse in that it is properly cognitive — it is the discourse of specialists, experts, advisers, and consultants, put to use in inquiries, reports, polls, indexes, statistics, and the like.

4. Once this information has been collected — as comprehensively as the nature of the enterprise will permit — a new genre of discourse is needed, where the stake is *What might we do?* Here Kant would see an idea of the imagination (intuition without concept), and Freud would see free association; we call it simulation, or montage of scenarios. Narrations of the unreal.

5. Deliberation in the strict sense of the term is concerned with these scenarios. It is subject to the regime of argumentation. Each party to the deliberation sets out to prove the other wrong, and show why. This is the genre Aristotle calls dialectics. Rhetoric is also involved. *Logoi,* or arguments, combine with *topoi,* or the classical steps of persuasion. The aim is not only to refute the other

but to persuade a third party (a judge, president, or electoral body in a democracy).

6. Then comes the moment of decision, that is, the moment of judgment: the most enigmatic of phrases, as Kant thought, the phrasing of the event par excellence. It can take the form of resolutions, programs, ballots, or arbitrations.

7. The judgment must be legitimated. This is the role of normative discourse (does one have the right to decide in this way?). Then it must be rendered executory (decrees, orders, laws, notices), and infractions must be punished.

This arrangement, despite appearances, is paradoxical in its linkages because of the heterogeneity of its components: how can a prescriptive phrase (*We ought to do this*) be deduced from a descriptive phrase (*This is what we can do*)? How can one link onto the prescription a normative phrase that will legitimate it? So, in this sense, there is a kind of fragility in the deliberative apparatus. The important role played by knowledge in this apparatus (technoscience at the service of politics) — when knowledge is itself subject to the continual deliberation of scientists — makes it still more fragile. But above all, the unity of the heterogeneous genres at play in this organization lies solely in the answer given to the first question: *What ought we to be?* This organization of the deliberative process is able to resist the separation of its elements only because it is a flow chart of the free will, of pure practical reason.

In the republic there is, by definition, a prevailing uncertainty about ends — an uncertainty about the identity of the *we*. As we have seen, the question of a final identity does not arise in the narrative tradition: the Cashinahua narrative always says that we ought to be what we are — Cashinahua.

(And the Aryan narrative says the same thing.) In the republic, there are many narratives because many final identities are possible; in despotism, there is only one because there is only one origin. The republic inspires not belief but reflection and judgment. It wills itself.

The grand narratives it needs are narratives of emancipation — they are not myths. Like myths, they fulfill a legitimating function: they legitimate social and political institutions and practices, forms of legislation, ethics, modes of thought, and symbolics. Yet unlike myths, they ground this legitimacy not in an original "founding" act, but in a future to be brought about, that is, in an Idea to realize. This Idea (of freedom, "enlightenment," socialism, general prosperity) has legitimating value because it is universal. It gives modernity its characteristic mode: the *project*, that is, the will directed toward a goal.

To elaborate this question, we would need to go back to Kant's historicopolitical opuscules; not just *An Answer to the Question: What Is Enlightenment?* but *Perpetual Peace, Idea for a Universal History within a Cosmopolitan Plan,* and especially the second *Conflict of the Faculties,* the conflict between philosophy and the faculty of law. I cannot do that here. The general sense we can draw from them is that the narrative of the universal history of humanity cannot be affirmed in mythical form; it must remain suspended from an Ideal of practical reason (freedom, emancipation). It cannot be verified by empirical proofs but only by indirect signs, *analoga,* which signal in experience that this ideal is present in people's minds. So any discussion of this history is "dialectical" in the Kantian sense, which is to say, without conclusion. The ideal is not presentable to the sensibility; the free society is no more demonstrable than the free act. And in the same way, there will always be a profound tension between what one ought to be and what one is.

Only one thing is certain: right cannot be de facto; real society draws legitimacy not from itself but from a community that is not properly nameable, merely required. One cannot deduce what a people ought to be from what it is today, nor can one deduce the concept of the universal citizen from its French or American name — only the reverse is possible. This is why, as I remarked earlier, the ferment and decomposition of the real community are inscribed in the principle of republicanism and in the history it develops. Sovereignty belongs not to the people but to the Idea of the free community. History simply marks the tension of this lack. The republic invokes freedom against security.

These brief reflections should make it possible, I think, to come to a better understanding of what the term totalitarianism implies. Evidently we ought to distinguish between the totalitarianism that turns its back on modern legitimation through the Idea of freedom and the totalitarianism that, on the contrary, issues from that Idea. Power can only draw its authority from a national or ethnic name (inscribed within a more or less fabulous corpus of stories, like the Germanic, Celtic, or Italic sagas) if it has completely broken with the legacy of the Declaration of Rights of 1789. It is not a case of "abandoning" the project of modernity, as Habermas has said with regard to postmodernity, but of the "liquidation" of that project. With this annihilation, an irreparable suspicion is engraved in European, if not Western, consciousness: that universal history does not move inevitably "toward the better," as Kant thought, or rather, that history does not necessarily have a universal finality. The authority of the proper name derives from the pragmatics of narration described above: I, Aryan, tell you Aryans the story of our Aryan ancestors as it was handed down to us. Listen to it, pass it on, execute it. This organization implies what I will call the exception. Aryans are the true men — the only ones. That which is not Aryan lives only because of a failure in the functioning of the vital principle. It is already dead. All that remains is to finish it off. The Nazi wars are sanitary operations, purifications. Nothing could be more foreign to republican legitimacy and the deliberative organization of discourse it demands, or, finally, to the idea of history it develops.

But things are not quite this simple. In the case of republicanism, the question of what the community ought to be and the answer given in the ideal of freedom do not deny that this community is already real. Rather they presuppose that it is, that it can name itself and honor this name in heroism, in "beautiful deaths." If we are to be citizens of the world, it is because we continue to be only French. We will always be French. This imbrication of authority with tradition and authority with the Idea can be clearly seen in an analysis of the Preamble to the Declaration of the Rights of Man of 1789, for example. Who, what y, could have the authority to declare the rights of man? There is an aporia of authorization. It is nonetheless surprising to find the name of an Assembly that represents a particular people, the French people, in the position of the legitimating instance, even though it places the declaration under the auspices of the Supreme Being. Why would the affirmation of a universal normative instance have universal value if a singular instance makes the declaration? How can one tell, afterward, whether the wars conducted by the singular instance in the name of the universal instance are wars of liberation or wars of conquest?

Equally, in the case of totalitarianism, the opposition to republicanism is not absolutely distinct. Nazism maintains the facade of a deliberative organization — parties, parliament — and it can even employ the republican epic of revolutionary wars to dress up the ethnocentrism of its conquests. (Hitler, with great ceremony, returned the ashes of Napoleon II [*l'Aiglon*] to the Invalides.) These things are parodies, of course. But what is their motive? To mask the reversal of legitimation. Despotism in this way recognizes the audience for republicanism. And indeed it needs that audience. A certain universalism persists in the logic of the exception when this logic is extended to include the whole of humanity.

The heart of this equivocation lies in the idea of the people. We are aware of the great value Nazism attached to it. The name of the people encompasses at once the singularity of a contingent community and the incarnation of a universal sovereignty. When one says *people*, it is impossible to tell exactly which identity one is talking about. When one puts the people, *das Volk*, in the place of the normative instance, it is impossible to tell whether the authority being invoked is despotic — summoning the tradition of an originary narrative — or if it is republican and appeals to the systematic institution of deliberation drawn to an Idea of freedom.

The peculiar importance Nazi politics placed in the mise-en-scène has often been noted. The aesthetics elaborated by postromanticism and Wagner (especially that of the "total work of art"), in which opera and cinema are privileged as "complete" arts, is put to the service of despotism, undermining the whole economy of the Schillerian project. Far from educating humanity and making it more receptive to Ideas, the sensible representation of the people to itself encourages it to identify itself as an exceptional singularity. Whether monumental or familiar in scale, the Nazi "festivals" exalt the Germanic identity by making symbolic figures from Aryan mythology sensible to the ear and eye. What is at work here is an art of persuasion that can only make a place for itself by eliminating the avant-gardist tendencies drawn to reflection.

This attempt at orthopedic figuration, elaborated and deployed by Nazism from the very beginning, only bore fruit because the German community was in the grip of a severe crisis of identity. This crisis, itself the culmination of the defeat of 1918, the settlement at Versailles, and the great socioeconomic depression of the 1930s, is often taken to be the cause of Nazism. But in any event, the idea of a cause is inappropriate in such matters. For our purposes, it is more interesting to remember that the identity crisis Nazism sought to cure — and which it merely succeeded in spreading to the rest of humanity — is potentially contained in the republican principle of legitimacy.

In *The Phenomenology of Spirit*, Hegel described the negativism of the modern ideal of freedom as a power capable of decomposing every concrete, singular objectivity, notably that of traditional institutions, and, I would add, that of every despotic community in Kant's sense — those communities that find the legitimacy of their modes of life in their name and their past. The dialectic of the particular and the universal, which Hegel gives the title of absolute freedom, can, he claims, end only in terror. For the ideal of absolute freedom, which is empty, any given reality must be suspected of being an obstacle to freedom. It has not been willed. Here I would say that the sole normative instance, the sole source of law, the sole y, is pure will — which is never this or that, never determined, but simply the potential to be all things. So it judges any particular act, even when it is prescribed by law and executed according to the rules, as failing to match up to the ideal. Terror acts on the suspicion that nothing is emancipated enough — and makes it into a politics. Every particular reality is a plot against the pure, universal will. Even the individual who occupies the

position of the normative instance is contingent in the light
of this ideal, and therefore suspect. Robespierre could have
no objection to his own execution, unless it was that his
judges were no less suspect than he was. " 'In whose name'
is the army being called in against the Assembly?'' he asks
Couthon on the eve of his death. The suppression of reality
through the death of suspects satisfies a logic that sees reality
as a plot against the Idea. And terror in this way plunges
the real community into despair about its identity. The
French no longer deserve the name of citizens when they
recoil in fear before the enormity of the crime by which they
sought to institute republican legitimacy. But in wanting
to be only French, the French renounce deliberation and
universal history, and renounce the ideal of freedom. The
Popular Front spreads fear across the land (and among the
Left), and the anti-Dreyfusard and Pétainist state brings
shame to the republicans (even the moderates).

As I see it, there should, in principle, be no confusion
between a politics of terror and the possible consequences
of despotic government, even though most of the time it
is not easy to make this distinction in historical reality. But
you only have to consider this: the normative instance has
to remain empty; any singularity (individual, family, party)
intending to occupy this place will be suspected of being
merely a usurper or impostor. The y who authorizes the
order and makes it law does not have a name — it is pure
will, unaffected by any determination and without ties to
any singularity. On whatever scale — a small Puritan community like Salem or the French nation — such an arrangement is highly likely to give rise to a politics of terror. And
a politics of terror, far from dispensing with deliberation
and its institutional organization, in fact demands it. For
this organization alone carries to the limit the responsibility

each person (as both representative and represented) has regarding each of the genres of discourse necessary for a political decision. What people put on the line in these deliberations is not only, and perhaps not essentially, their lives: it is their judgment, their responsibility in the face of the event. We should remember that, in principle, a complex deliberative organization leaves open the way that one phrase or genre of discourse is linked to another. This is true at every step in the process of the will.

The republic is, in its very constitution, attentive to the event. What we call freedom is this alertness to what can happen, which must be judged outside of any rule. Terror is one way of accounting for the indeterminacy of what is happening. Philosophy is another. The difference between them lies in the time set aside for collecting information and making judgments. Philosophy takes its time, as they say. Urgency hastens republican decision making — and political decision making generally.

Totalitarianism would consist in subjecting institutions legitimated by the Idea of freedom to legitimation by myth. Although clearly despotic in the Kantian sense, it borrows its universalizing power from republicanism. It is not simply *Let us become what we are — Aryans,* but *Let the whole of humanity be Aryan.* Once named, the singular *we* then has the pretension of imparting its name to the end pursued by human history. In this sense totalitarianism is modern. It needs not only the people, but the decomposition of the people into "masses" in search of an identity by means of parties authorized by the republic. If it is to overturn the republic, totalitarianism needs democracy's equivocation.

I would also distinguish Nazi totalitarianism from Stalinist totalitarianism. The Stalinist mode of legitimation is, in principle, still republican. Socialism is one version of the narrative of universal emancipation born of the Declaration of the Rights of Man. The First International takes its authority from a declaration of the rights of the universal worker. Communism is a philosophy of human history. Its internationalism plainly meant that it would never recognize the legitimacy of any local powers, which, being particular, are necessarily despotic. An enormous effort was made to give the universal proletariat a reality beyond that of working classes still bound to national traditions and differential claims. That this effort failed, that Bolshevism, like Stalinism, was to become the very incarnation of chauvinism, does not mean that the mode of legitimation of Soviet power was ever in principle a slogan like *Let us be Russian* or *Let humanity be Russian*. Again in principle, the idea of the people was itself subject to a radical critique in Marxism, in the concept of class struggle. Marxism thus significantly accelerated the decomposition of the particular nominal community, and did so in the spirit of workers' republicanism.

The question I am asking is whether Stalinism is not a politics of despotism so much as a politics of terror. The analyses sketched out here lead me to just this conclusion. The very decomposition of Russian civil society by the Stalinist and post-Stalinist apparatus supports this hypothesis. It has no equivalent in Nazism. Nazism, on the contrary, provided a solid and durable structure to accommodate the modes of life and socioeconomic reality of Germany, in conformity with the despotic principle — and this is what has in Germany engendered a feeling of guilt unknown in communist nations. The Stalinist terror was able to deceive people as long as it did because it seemed to be working toward the realization of the socialist republic. Its authority came from Bolshevism, the Marxist cousin of Enlightenment Jacobinism. It has taken almost half a century for this imposture to be exposed. In those nations that have, as a result of imperialism, suffered an identity crisis analogous to Germany's in the 1930s, it has still not exhausted its powers of deception. And it is still the case that in every so-called communist country the normative instance authorizes the law only by setting it against those to whom it applies. The normative instance cannot invoke the life of the people or the conservation of people's origins and identity. It cannot rule by true despotism, the despotism of singularity. But conversely, it can no longer claim to take its authority from an infinite process of emancipation without provoking the laughter or tears of those it oppresses — it has been a long time since its terror was republican. People in these countries know what bureaucratic power is — the delegitimation of the legislator.

I have said nothing about capitalism. There is just one thing I would like to suggest to you. The principle that *any* object and *any* action are acceptable (permitted) so long as they can enter into economic exchange is not totalitarian in a political sense. But in terms of language it is, since it calls for the complete hegemony of the economic genre of discourse. The simple canonical formula of this genre is: *I will let you have this, if you in return can let me have that.* Among its other attributes, this genre always calls for new *thises* to enter into exchange (today, for example, techno-scientific knowledge) and uses payment as a means of neutralizing their power as events. Evidently market expansion has nothing to do with the universality of republicanism. Capital does not need deliberation either politically or economically. But socially it does, because it needs civil society in order to repeat its cycle. Society is for capital the indispensable moment of the destruction (consumption) of singular *thises* or *thats*.

An examination of the present status of capitalism from the point of view of totalitarianism would be extremely useful. Capitalism accommodates the republican institution, but cannot cope with terror (which destroys the market). It gets along well with despotism (as we saw with Nazism). It is hardly bothered by the decline of the grand narratives of universality (including the liberal narrative of humanity's increasing prosperity). Capital, it could be said, does not need legitimation: it prescribes nothing, in the strict sense of obligation, and consequently has no need to cite an instance to make a prescription normative. Capital is present everywhere, but as necessity rather than finality. We can, I think, understand why it seems like necessity if we analyze the canonical formula of the genre of discourse peculiar to it. We would see that behind this appearance there is still a hidden finality: gaining time. Is this a universally valid end?

Chapter 5

Dispatch concerning the Confusion of Reasons

To Jacques Enaudeau
Paris, May 25, 1984

The term *reason* is truly vast. Suppose I limit its reach. I shall restrict myself to its "use" in what has been defined as science since the time of Galileo. Within these boundaries, we can call reason the collection of rules that a discourse must respect when it sets out to know an object (the referent) and to make it known. I do not feel that "today" marks any great change in the rules observed by scientific discourse. The proliferation of axiomatics (systems of operators) over several centuries is a sign not of less reason but of a greater rigor within reason. In particular, the axiomatics of traditional scientific languages (arithmetic, geometry) have been reformulated as far as possible. But in this instance, the formal rules required of a language of knowledge, its "reason," are merely made more explicit. Propositions must still be "correctly formed"; the operators used in demonstrations must still be differentiated and fully explained; and, in "objective" sciences, the administration of the "proof" of a claim must still include the means of effecting and repeating the observation. Like everybody else, I realize this does not have much to do with the scientist's "experience" in the laboratory. This experience is very important in its own sphere and deserving of anthropological study — but it is only one consideration. Quite another matter, and a strictly discursive one, is the collection of rules (the regime) that, if not observed, suffice to exclude a discourse from knowledge in the strict sense of the term. For example, the interpretation of a dream in psychoanalysis does not obey cognitive rules, since the "given" (the account of the dream) cannot be reproduced as exactly as one would wish and is therefore not universally accessible. The same applies to the hypothesis on the first second of the big bang, if we are to believe Michel Cassé.

I am talking here about scientific discourse in its essential difference from every other genre of discourse. Scientific discourse has to be distinguished from those discourses that take it as their object. It is in these discourses — "epistemological" in the most general sense — that the idea of scientific reason reflects upon itself, elaborates, modifies, and ideologizes itself. Commentaries on science have multiplied since the age of Galileo. There is now a (sociological) science of science, a psychoanalysis of science (as *libido sciendi*), a history of scientific "paradigms," and so forth. All assume that scientific reason is not independent of empirical variables — whether technical, social, psychical, or imaginary. Despite frequent confusion on this point, however, it is the *content* of scientific discourse, not its *regime*, that is affected by such dependence. Since our hypothesis is that cognitive reason lies in the rules of language games, I will ignore this aspect of it here.

More relevant is the issue of the *status* of these rules. "Today," it is in examining this second aspect of scientific reason that commentary provokes a feeling of greater uncertainty. In questioning the status of the rules of knowledge, we question the origin of these rules: Are they given, natural, divine, or necessary? And if they are, is it within reason's power to deduce or even describe their creation? Or isn't it possible that, on the contrary, their creation must always escape reason in an inevitable *circulus vitiosus?* When we ask the reason for rules, we are asking the reason of reason. Classicism was metaphysical in that it provided this primary reason. Modernity, or at least *one* modernity (that of Augustine and Kant), is critical — it elaborates finitude; it gives the reason that prohibits reasoning about the foundation of reasoning. Postmodernity would instead be empiricocritical or pragmatic — the reason of reason cannot be given without producing the circle, but the capacity to formulate new rules (axiomatics) appears whenever the "need" is felt. Science would be a *means of revealing reason,* reason itself remaining the raison d'être of science.

The status thus assigned to reason is borrowed directly from technicist ideology (the dialectic of needs and means, an indifference to origins, the postulate of an infinite capacity for "novelty," and legitimation by superior power). Scientific reason is not examined according to the (cognitive) criterion of truth or falsity, on the message/referent axis, but according to the performativity of its utterances, on the (pragmatic) axis of addressor/addressee. What I say has more truth than what you say, since I can "do more" (gain more time, go further) with what I say than you can with what you say. A minor consequence of this displacement is that the best-equipped laboratory has a better chance of being right. So is right in fact might?

The conglomeration that Habermas calls technoscience is not only an established state of affairs, it is a state of reason. The scholar used to be regarded as having a vocation; the scientist is now regarded as a professional in the process of deprofessionalization. We know that every profession is in danger of collapsing when another end is imposed on it, an end replacing or supplementing its "proper" end — a hegemonic end, even if it is initially only appended to it. What Smith and Marx said about the ex-weavers of Antwerp of the fifteenth century, when the law of mercantile capital forced them into the factories — doesn't this also apply today to ex-scholars who are subject to a regime of maximum performativity, not simply to the means they have at their disposal, but to the very ends to which they can be "habilitated"? (Take a look at the reasons listed in the recent decrees for the reform of undergraduate studies in France.)

It will be said that this collapse of the cognitive profession may in some respects be a good thing, as was said of the collapse of the weavers' profession. Isn't the former the price we have to pay for the development of knowledge, just as the latter was for clothing and living conditions? This could be argued (by emphasizing the accelerating pace of discovery and invention in the large laboratories), but only if we accept the comparability of the two occupations without question. But supposing we accept this, it is still true that the occupation of learning today can no more find its legitimacy, reason, or end, in itself, than could the occupation of manufacturing synthetic textiles. The scientific worker would "know" things in order to earn a living, the employer would "make things known" in order to make money. If we were to give the reason of cognitive reason, we would be designating the end pursued by capitalism. And to object that the use of cognitive skills should in fact belong to public institutions simply means that the reason of knowledge should be sought in the end pursued by these institutions or their proxies, not in knowledge itself.

In all these cases, the reason of cognitive reason would inscribe itself in the social, economic, and political order. Science would offer greater justice, greater well-being, and greater freedom. This was largely the thinking of Europe and North America two centuries ago when they gave credence to the grand narratives of emancipation in the Enlightenment.

A large share of the crimes (or at least the deceptions) that make up the history of the last two centuries, and much of the grief that marks the end of the twentieth century, should perhaps be attributed to the cohabitation of these two orders (which Pascal distinguished absolutely from one another): knowledge and the "world." When Paul Feyerabend, for instance, demands a separation of science and state, he is rightly attacking the confusion of reasons, the reason of state and the reason of knowledge. They are incommensurable, as incommensurable as the reason of state and the "raison d'être" (sometimes called honor or ethics) that can move a citizen, or a lover, to prefer death to living as a Nazi, or living with betrayal.

There is no reasonable excuse for the confusion of reasons. The confusion lies in the very "modern" project of a universal language, that is, a metalanguage capable of collecting together every shred of meaning established in specific languages. The doubt cast on "reason" springs not from the sciences but from the critique of metalanguage, that is, from the decline of metaphysics (and therefore of meta-politics as well).

This situation indicates the stake confronting philosophical thought today. We must follow metaphysics in its fall, as Adorno said, but without lapsing into the current mood of positivist pragmatism, which, beneath its liberal exterior, is no less hegemonic than dogmatism. We must trace a line of resistance to both of them. We must counter-attack the confusions without forming a new "front." For the time being, the defense of reasons is conducted by "micrologies."

Chapter 6

Postscript to Terror and the Sublime

To Augustin Nancy
Berlin, January 5, 1985

In his essay "Dialectics or Decomposition: Postmodernity or Modernity," Gérard Raulet grapples with the relationships that he attempts to set up between modernity, postmodernity, and the aesthetic of the sublime. A small rejoinder is indicated.

According to Raulet, when I oppose the Kantian sublime (founded on the incommensurability of the faculties) to the Hegelian dialectic (which totalizes them), I find myself unable to suggest any antidote to totalitarianism other than a politics of terror. It would be useful to disentangle these two equations: speculative discourse = totalitarianism; philosophy of the sublime = terror. This I tried to do in some detail in *The Differend*, in a "Memorandum on Legitimation" and in a study entitled "Le Nom et l'exception" (unpublished). Here, I would simply like to remind you of why these identifications are unacceptable.

Hegelian speculative discourse, which is built on the principle of the *"Result,"* the cumulation of experience (in *The Phenomenology*) or moments of being (in the *Encyclopedia*), stems from the transcendental illusion detected by critical philosophy. When speculative discourse is transposed — is it even transposed? — into politics, Raulet writes that "it realizes totalitarianism," the presence of the Idea in experience. I do not agree with this inference. To authorize its law, the totalitarian state (whose paradigm is Nazi power) makes no appeal to the task of achieving an idea in reality or of bringing spirit to freedom and self-consciousness — at least for those who believe in the return to myth that it demands. Its appeal is to an inverse legitimacy, to the authority of roots and of a race placed at the origin of the Western epoch, a race that "only" has to get rid of its parasites before reemerging in its primordial purity. This is why the "law" of Nazi totalitarianism is a law of exclusion, exception, and extermination. An ailing identity has to be restored to health. This would never apply to a Hegelian politics (if there were such a thing). The propagation, propaganda, and war that characterize Nazi expansionism are of course reminiscent of revolutionary struggles for the liberation of peoples. That is because in totalitarianism an ideal inherited from modernity persists, even though it is disavowed — the ideal of the universalization of values: not only will Germanity be "pure," but so will all of humanity. All the same, Hitler is not Hegel. Hegel would be Napoleon: the new world reconciled with the old. With Hitler, the new world is foreclosed in the restoration of the archaic.

As for terror, the Hegelian analysis of absolute freedom taken up by Raulet is in fact a direct attack on a politics of pure practical reason, which, if it existed, would be called a politics of the sublime or by the sublime. But in my opinion this attack is misdirected.

What engenders terror is not, as Hegel claims, the criminal impatience felt by a universalist ethics when confronted by the derisory obstacle of singular givens. It is the interminable suspicion that each consciousness can harbor about any object, including itself; the suspicion that even that act or judgment that appears to have universal import, and to have a genuine wish to legislate with a view to a community of free beings, is perhaps motivated by empirical interests and singular passions.

Hegelianism describes terror the same way it attacks Kantian ethics, by the usual device: clean hands mean no hands. To place any credence in this commonplace is not to have read Kant. Conversely, the suspicion cast on disinterestedness directly concerns the Kantian problematic of the "abyss" between the faculties. The ethical genre and, before it, the dialectical genre (in the first *Critique*) are heterogeneous with respect to the cognitive genre, whose transcendental conditions are laid out in the first Analytic. The Transcendental Deduction demonstrates that prescription and knowledge (or dialectical *disputatio* — dispute — and knowledge) obey entirely different rules. But the abyss is not of a kind that would make transcendental appearance impossible or suspicion ill founded. On the contrary (and this is described in the discussion of the third Antinomy, for example), they are both inevitable if the same object "accepts" being caught within two heterogeneous genres. An act or a judgment can lay claim to ethical universality (in aiming to legislate for a community of free and rational beings) and *at the same time* constitute the object of what we might call positive knowledge, as a phenomenon (social, psychological, etc.) involved in a chain of determinations of cause and effect — in other words, empirically motivated.

This uncertainty, which gives rise to suspicion, is the result of the incommensurability of genres (or faculties) combined with the uniqueness of an object or "territory" (in human, anthropological experience).

The full force of critique comes down on the dividing line between the genres. But it is not the same thing to have suspicions about the confusion of reasons, in order to examine them and establish their respective legitimacies, as it is to set the political police on the trail of impure motives.

There can be no confusion between Jacobin suspicion and the suspicions of critique. In the history of ideas and practices, Jacobin suspicion is related to the grave philosophical uncertainty that governs the thought of Rousseau, an uncertainty that is precisely *not critical* — notably, his hesitation or confusion between a (pure) general will and the (empirical) will of all, that is, between the republic and the democracy (to return to the fundamental distinction Kant draws in the second section of *Perpetual Peace*). It is this confusion that tilts the course of democracy toward terror: a confusion discernible in *The Social Contract* and manifest in the politics of the Jacobin government.

Kant clearly identified the danger of confusing transcendental freedom (an Idea that is unpresentable, scarcely even conceivable) with "empirical freedom" (if there is such a thing). No *fact* in experience could attest to the truth of a speculative argument (for example, that there is a tendency toward the better in the history of humanity). For Ideas, there are no presentable objects — there are only *analoga*, signs, hypotyposes. And so it is for the finality of human history, as it is described in the *Idea for a Universal History within a Cosmopolitan Plan*.

As for the French Republic (since Raulet pits me against Jacobinism), the second *Conflict of the Faculties*, written after the Terror in 1797, explains that although the reality of the

Terror (its empirical factuality) cannot of course be recognized as legitimate on an ethical or even political level, at least in its effect it is a sign of humanity's progress toward the better. This effect is the enthusiasm (paragraph 6) felt by the peoples of the world upon hearing news of it.

That enthusiasm, the enthusiasm of the spectators, cannot be suspected of being particular (like aesthetic feeling, it requires unanimity in principle), nor of being interested (people under the yoke of despotism have nothing to gain by making this feeling public). Considered as a passion, it has no ethical value (only respect for the moral law is an ethically pure feeling). But, as an extreme case of sublime affection, its value as a political sign is undeniable according to Kant. For the experience of the sublime feeling demands a sensitivity to Ideas that is not natural but acquired through culture. Humanity must be cultivated (and thus in a state of progress) to be able to feel, even in the crime perpetrated by the Jacobins, the "presence" of the unpresentable Idea of freedom.

As for a politics of the sublime, there is no such thing. It could only be terror. But there is an aesthetic of the sublime in politics. Actors or heroes in the political drama are always suspect, and always should be suspected of pursuing particular and interested motives. But the sublime affection the public experiences for the drama is not to be suspected. On the basis of this problematic we would have to elaborate the (often noted) affinity between the revolution and theater, along with the kinds of "manipulation" and cynicism that it invites (in Nazism, specifically) and the innocence that it can bring with it (as we saw in 1968).

Let me make a few more remarks, without hoping to elaborate fully the problems posed. Gérard Raulet reproaches "my" postmodernism for being as "impotent" in the face of totalitarianism as Weimar avant-gardism was when confronted with the rise of Nazism.

1. It is simplistic to use one term (totalitarianism) to cover both Nazism and capitalism in its postmodern phase. Both perhaps take possession of the totality of life. But Nazism does so openly, under the regime of the "will" (or the faculty of desire), and therefore politically, by fixing its gaze on the source of its legitimacy, the *Völkisches*. Capitalism does so of necessity, as a matter of course (the fact of the world market), without any concern for legitimation, by pursuing the disintegration of the modern social bond, the community of citizens. Even if the line of resistance seems identical in each case (in avant-gardism, this remains unclear) it would hardly have the same impact. Nazism burns, assassinates, and exiles the avant-gardes; capitalism isolates them, speculates on them, and delivers them muzzled to the culture industry. What is "impotent" in one case is not necessarily so in the other.

2. As for this "impotence" to which we would be doomed with and by "my" postmodernism — thought takes a long time. I sense in Raulet a haste to conclude, a desire to think quickly. I do not propose an "intellectual party"; I write its epitaph [*son* Tombeau]. I do not bury it, as Blanchot might like to think. The decline of modern ideas, which Adorno analyzed in *Negative Dialectics*, entails a vacancy of the place once occupied by intellectuals (in the style of Zola). Consider the tragic errors befalling those unwilling to acknowledge the gravity of the crisis: Sartre, Chomsky, Negri, Foucault. And don't laugh. These misjudgments must be inscribed in the tableau of postmodernity. The avant-gardes' unremitting work of anamnesis has, for a hundred years, saved the honor of thought, if not of humanity, without compromise and everywhere. It is not enough but it is something.

3. My "irrationalism." Imagine . . . I've struggled in different ways against capitalism's regime of pseudorationality and performativity. I've emphasized the importance of the moment of dissent in the process of constructing knowledge, lying at the heart of the community of thought. Thus its avant-gardism, and in that sense its fidelity to the essential character of Aristotelian and Kantian dialectics, and its affinity to Feyerabend. A few months ago I sent to your young friend Jacques a short dispatch on the confusion of reasons. People who invoke "Reason" perpetuate the confusion. We must take care to distinguish different reasons: the reason pertaining to phenomena, the reason able to legitimate a political regime, the reason allowing each person to live with his or her own singularity, the reason that says a work is admirable, and also the reason why there is a duty, or a debt. Making such distinctions is the activity of critical rationalism. They lay the foundations for what Adorno saw as a "politics" of micrologies. They trace an immediate line of resistance to the current "totalitarianism."

Chapter 7

Note on the Meaning of "Post-"

To Jessamyn Blau
Milwaukee, May 1, 1985

I would like to pass on to you a few thoughts that are merely intended to raise certain problems concerning the term "postmodern," without wanting to resolve them. By doing this, I do not want to close the debate but rather to situate it, in order to avoid confusion and ambiguity. I have just three points to make.

First, the opposition between postmodernism and modernism, or the modern movement (1910–45) in architecture. According to Portoghesi, the rupture of postmodernism consists in an abrogation of the hegemony of Euclidean geometry (its sublimation in the plastic poetics of "de Stijl," for example). To follow Gregotti, the difference between modernism and postmodernism would be better characterized by the following feature: the disappearance of the close bond that once linked the project of modern architecture to an ideal of the progressive realization of social and individual emancipation encompassing all humanity. Postmodern architecture finds itself condemned to undertake a series of minor modifications in a space inherited from modernity, condemned to abandon a global reconstruction of the space of human habitation. The perspective then opens onto a vast landscape, in the sense that there is no longer any horizon of universality, universalization, or general emancipation to greet the eye of postmodern man, least of all the eye of the architect. The disappearance of the Idea that rationality and freedom are progressing would explain a "tone," style, or mode specific to postmodern architecture. I would say it is a sort of "bricolage": the multiple quotation of elements taken from earlier styles or periods, classical and modern; disregard for the environment; and so on.

One point about this perspective is that the "post-" of postmodernism has the sense of a simple succession, a diachronic sequence of periods in which each one is clearly identifiable. The "post-" indicates something like a conversion: a new direction from the previous one.

Now this idea of a linear chronology is itself perfectly "modern." It is at once part of Christianity, Cartesianism, and Jacobinism: since we are inaugurating something completely new, the hands of the clock should be put back to zero. The very idea of modernity is closely correlated with the principle that it is both possible and necessary to break with tradition and institute absolutely new ways of living and thinking.

We now suspect that this "rupture" is in fact a way of forgetting or repressing the past, that is, repeating it and not surpassing it.

I would say that, in the "new" architecture, the quotation of motifs taken from earlier architectures relies on a procedure analogous to the way dream work uses diurnal residues left over from life past, as outlined by Freud in *The Interpretation of Dreams (Traumdeutung)*. This destiny of repetition and quotation — whether it is taken up ironically, cynically, or naively — is in any event obvious if we think of the tendencies that at present dominate painting, under the names of transavantgardism, neoexpressionism, and so forth. I will return to this a bit later.

This departure from architectural "postmodernism" leads me to a second connotation of the term "postmodern" (and I have to admit that I am no stranger to its misunderstanding).

The general idea is a trivial one. We can observe and establish a kind of decline in the confidence that, for two centuries, the West invested in the principle of a general progress in humanity. This idea of a possible, probable, or necessary progress is rooted in the belief that developments made in the arts, technology, knowledge, and freedoms would benefit humanity as a whole. It is true that ascertaining the identity of the subject who suffered most from a lack of development — the poor, the worker, or the illiterate — continued to be an issue throughout the nineteenth and twentieth centuries. As you know, there was controversy and even war between liberals, conservatives, and "leftists" over the true name to be given to the subject whose emancipation required assistance. Yet all these tendencies were united in the belief that initiatives, discoveries, and institutions only had legitimacy insofar as they contributed to the emancipation of humanity.

After two centuries we have become more alert to signs that would indicate an opposing movement. Neither liberalism (economic and political) nor the various Marxisms have emerged from these bloodstained centuries without attracting accusations of having perpetrated crimes against humanity. We could make a list of proper names — places, people, dates — capable of illustrating or substantiating our suspicions. Following Theodor Adorno, I have used the name "Auschwitz" to signify just how impoverished recent Western history seems from the point of view of the "modern" project of the emancipation of humanity. What kind of thought is capable of "relieving" Auschwitz — relieving (*relever*) in the sense of *aufheben* — capable of situating it in a general, empirical, or even speculative process directed toward universal emancipation? There is a sort of grief in the *Zeitgeist*. It can find expression in reactive, even reactionary, attitudes or in utopias — but not in a positive orientation that would open up a new perspective.

Technoscientific development has become a means of deepening the malaise rather than allaying it. It is no longer possible to call development progress. It seems to proceed of its own accord, with a force, an autonomous motoricity that is independent of us. It does not answer to demands issuing from human needs. On the contrary, human entities — whether social or individual — always seem destabilized by the results and implications of development. I am thinking of its intellectual and mental results as well as its material results. We could say that humanity's condition has become one of chasing after the process of the accumulation of new objects (both of practice and of thought).

As you might imagine, understanding the reason for this process of complexification is an important question for me — an obscure question. We could say there exists a sort of destiny, or involuntary destination toward a condition that is increasingly complex. The needs for security, identity, and happiness springing from our immediate condition as living beings, as social beings, now seem irrelevant next to this sort of constraint to complexify, mediatize, quantify, synthesize, and modify the size of each and every object. We are like Gullivers in the world of technoscience: sometimes too big, sometimes too small, but never the right size. From this perspective, the insistence on simplicity generally seems today like a pledge to barbarism.

On this same point, the following issue also has to be elaborated. Humanity is divided into two parts. One faces the challenge of complexity, the other that ancient and terrible challenge of its own survival. This is perhaps the most important aspect of the failure of the modern project — a project that, need I remind you, once applied in principle to the whole of humanity.

I will give my third point — the most complex — the shortest treatment. The question of postmodernity is also, or first of all, a question of expressions of thought: in art, literature, philosophy, politics.

We know that in the domain of art, for example, or more precisely in the visual and plastic arts, the dominant view today is that the great movement of the avant-gardes is over and done with. It has, as it were, become the done thing to indulge or deride the avant-gardes — to regard them as the expression of an outdated modernity.

I do not like the term avant-garde, with its military connotations, any more than anyone else. But I do observe that the true process of avant-gardism was in reality a kind of work, a long, obstinate, and highly responsible work concerned with investigating the assumptions implicit in modernity. I mean that for a proper understanding of the work of modern painters, from, say, Manet to Duchamp or Barnett Newman, we would have to compare their work with anamnesis, in the sense of a psychoanalytic therapy. Just as patients try to elaborate their current problems by freely associating apparently inconsequential details with past situations — allowing them to uncover hidden meanings in their lives and their behavior — so we can think of the work of Cézanne, Picasso, Delaunay, Kandinsky, Klee, Mondrian, Malevich, and finally Duchamp as a working through (*durch-arbeiten*) performed by modernity on its own meaning.

If we abandon that responsibility, we will surely be condemned to repeat, without any displacement, the West's "modern neurosis" — its schizophrenia, paranoia, and so on, the source of the misfortunes we have known for two centuries.

You can see that when it is understood in this way, the "post-" of "postmodern" does not signify a movement of *comeback, flashback,* or *feedback,* that is, not a movement of repetition but a procedure in "ana-": a procedure of analysis, anamnesis, anagogy, and anamorphosis that elaborates an "initial forgetting."

Chapter 8

Ticket for a New Stage

To Thomas Chaput
Rome, April 12, 1985

The thought and action of the nineteenth and twentieth centuries are ruled by the Idea of the emancipation of humanity. This Idea develops at the end of the eighteenth century in the philosophy of the Enlightenment and in the French Revolution. The progress of the sciences, technologies, the arts, and political freedoms will liberate the whole of humanity from ignorance, poverty, backwardness, despotism. Not only will it produce happy people, but, thanks to education in particular, it will also produce enlightened citizens, masters of their own destiny.

From this source spring all the political currents of the last two centuries, with the exception of traditional reaction and Nazism. The sometimes violent divergences between political liberalism, economic liberalism, Marxism, anarchism, the radicalism of the Third Republic and socialism, count for little next to the abiding unanimity about the end to be attained. The promise of freedom is for everyone the horizon of progress and its legitimation. Everyone is moving or thinks they are moving toward a humanity transparent to itself, toward a world citizenry.

These ideals are on the wane in general attitudes in what we call developed nations. The discourse of the political class continues to use the rhetoric of emancipation. But it does not seem able to heal the wounds inflicted on the "modern" ideal over some two centuries of history. It was not a lack of progress but, on the contrary, development (technoscientific, artistic, economic, political) that created the possibility of total war, totalitarianisms, the growing gap between the wealth of the North and the impoverished South, unemployment and the "new poor," general deculturation and the crisis in education (in the transmission of knowledge), and the isolation of the artistic avant-gardes (and for a while now, their repudiation).

We can put names to all of these wounds. They are strewn across the field of our unconscious like so many secret obstacles to the tranquil perpetuation of the "project of modernity." On the pretext of safeguarding this project, men and women of my generation in Germany have, for forty years, enforced a silence on their children about the "Nazi interlude." This interdiction of anamnesis serves as a symbol for the whole of the West. Can there be progress without anamnesis? Anamnesis, by way of a painful elaboration, allows us to elaborate our mourning for attachments and affections of every sort, for the loves and terrors associated with these names. It impressed me that the federal authorities would allow a trench to be carved into the immaculate lawn of the Mall in Washington, somber and lit by candles, with the name "Vietnam Veterans Memorial." For a moment we sink into a vague, fin de siècle melancholy that is apparently inexplicable.

But this decline of the "project of modernity" is not decadence. It is accompanied by the quasi-exponential development of technoscience. Now there is not, and never again will there be, a loss or diminution of knowledge and expertise, even if it means destroying humanity. This is an original situation in history. It expresses an ancient truth that strikes us today with particular force. Scientific or technical discovery was never subordinate to demands arising from human needs. It was always driven by a dynamic independent of the things people might judge desirable, profitable, or comfortable. And we are able to put faith in the development of expertise and knowledge precisely because our desire for them is incommensurable with the demand for profit. There is always some delay in humanity's capacity to understand the "ideas" and to act on the "means" that result from inventions, discoveries, research, and happenstance.

Three remarkable events are taking place today: first, the fusion of technology and science in the immense technoscientific network; second, across all the sciences, the revision not simply of hypotheses or even "paradigms" but of the modes of reasoning and logic once considered "natural" or imprescriptible — paradoxes abound in the theories of mathematics, physics, astrophysics, and biology; finally, the qualitative transformation brought about by new technology — the most recent generation of machines can perform operations of memory, reference, calculation, grammar, rhetoric and poetics, reasoning and judgment (expertise). They are prostheses of language, that is to say, prostheses of thought. And though still rudimentary, they will reach a level of sophistication in the coming decades such that their applications [*logiciels*] will be able to match the complex logic used in the most advanced research.

It is clear now, after the event, that the works produced by the artistic avant-gardes for more than a century are involved in a parallel process of complexification. This complexification bears on the sensibilities (sight, hearing, movement, language), not on expertise or knowledge. But the philosophical import of these works, or their power of reflection if you like, is as far-reaching in the order of receptivity and "taste" as is the import of technoscience in matters of knowledge and practice.

So it is this growing complexity in most domains, including "ways of life" or everyday life, that I am sketching as the horizon for your century. And a crucial task is circumscribed by this situation: to make humanity adept at adapting itself to ways of feeling, understanding, and acting that, in their extreme complexity, exceed its requirements. At a minimum, this task implies a resistance to simplism and simplifying slogans, to calls for clearness and straightforwardness, and to desires for a return to solid values. Simplification is already starting to look barbarous or reactive. The "political class" will have to (already has to) reckon with this exigency if it is to avoid sinking into decrepitude and dragging humanity down with it as it goes.

The new stage is slowly being set. Some of the highlights: the cosmos is the fallout from an explosion; the force of the original shock is still scattering the debris; as they burn, the stars transmute the elements; their time is running out; so is the sun's; the chances of a synthesis of the first algae occurring in water on earth were minuscule; the human being is even less probable; its cortex is the most complex material organization that we know; the machines this cortex engenders are its extensions; the network these machines will form will be like a second and even more complex cortex; the network will have to solve the problem of evacuating humanity to another place before the death of the sun; the selection of those who can go and those who will be left to face the implosion has already started — according to the criterion of "underdevelopment."

A final blow to humanity's narcissism: it is at the service of complexification. At this very moment the stage is being set in the unconscious of the young. In your own.

Chapter 9

Gloss on Resistance

To David Rogozinski
Prague, June 21, 1985

In a text entitled ''Le Corps interposé'' (you will find it in *Passé-Présent*, April 3, 1984), Claude Lefort considers Orwell's *1984* from two main perspectives.

Lefort, unlike most commentators, refuses to ignore the very writing of the book. Orwell does not put forward a theoretical critique of bureaucracy. This novel of totalitarianism in action does not set out to be a political theory. Orwell, in writing a literary work, suggests that the genre of criticism is incapable of resisting the coercive sway of bureaucracy. There is instead an affinity or complicity between them. Both attempt to exercise complete control over their respective domains. But literary writing, artistic writing, because it demands privation [*dénuement*], cannot cooperate with a project of domination or total transparency, even involuntarily.

In Orwell, this resistance is first inscribed, conspicuously, in the novelistic genre and narrative mode peculiar to *1984*. The world of Big Brother is not analyzed but recounted. Now, as Walter Benjamin has observed, the narrator is always implicated in the story that is told, while on principle the theoretician should not be implicated in the conceptual elaboration of an object.

In *1984*, the narration is so closely bound up with the story that the author of the novel is supplanted by the author of the private diary. From the pen of the hero, Winston, writing his diary, the world of consummate bureaucracy is delivered to Orwell's reader burdened by mundane worries, reduced to the frame of a subjective life that will never take in the totality, infiltrated by daydreams, dreams, and phantasms, in other words, by the most singular formations of the unconscious.

The decision to write a diary is an initial act of resistance. Yet the text being written in hiding shows that Winston's secret universe, which is unknown to him and which he partly discovers by writing, is not repressed by the bureaucratic order from the outside. In the very process of revealing itself to the author of the diary, this secret universe is trapped by the bureaucratic order. And it is ultimately exploited by it, precisely in the sense that the information is exploited for affinities, unforeseen vulnerabilities, and lapses embodied in Winston's love for Julia, who loves him, and in his friendship for O'Brien, who spies on him and betrays him.

As Lefort points out, in illuminating this zone where the private and the public overlap, Orwell's narrative reveals that the exercise of domination is only total when it enters

into symbiosis with the singular passions of those it oppresses, and that the key weakness it uses to secure their
surrender is not the fear of death, but the secret terrors that
are the price each person, individually, must have paid and
must pay to become human.

That said — and here I am expanding a little on Claude
Lefort's commentary for you — it is one thing to conceive
of this sort of insinuation of the master in the slave, quite
another to make it felt. For the reader to feel it, a representation or picture of it would not be enough. The combination of resistance and weakening must occur in the very act
of writing. Writing must perform on itself — in its detail,
in the restlessness of words that appear or fail to appear,
in its receptivity to the contingency of the word [*verbe*] —
the very work of exploring its own weakness and energy
that Winston's labor performs in the face of the insidious
threat of totalitarianism.

The adversary and accomplice of writing, its Big Brother
(or rather O'Brien), is language: by this I mean not only
the mother tongue but the whole inheritance of words,
phrases, and works that we call literary culture. One writes
against language, but necessarily with it. To say what it
already knows how to say is not writing. One wants to say
what it does not know how to say, but what one imagines
it should be able to say. One violates it, one seduces it, one
introduces into it an idiom unknown to it. When this desire
disappears — this desire for it to be able to say something
other than what it already knows how to say — when language is felt to be impenetrable and inert, rendering all
writing vain, it is called Newspeak.

One might wonder whether this unconditional surrender
of writing to language is even possible. Even to describe
this extenuated state of writing, its "1984," one still has to
write, and put on the line, one more time, the double resis-

tance of the already said to the not yet said, of words that want to appear to words that are laid down.

The impossibility of eluding the moment of writing results in an aporia. Even when totalitarianism has won, when it occupies the whole terrain, it is not fully realized unless it has eliminated the uncontrollable contingency of writing. So totalitarianism must renounce writing — writing as I am trying to define it (following others). But if totalitarianism remains unwritten, it cannot be total. On the other hand, should it attempt to be written, it would have to concede that with writing there is at least one region where restlessness, lack, and "idiocy" come out into the open. And by conceding this, it gives up any hope of incarnating the totality, or even of controlling it.

What is at stake in this aporia is the fate befalling the event. Like theory, which, hypothetically, keeps its head above the water of time, totalitarian bureaucracy likes to keep the event under its thumb. When something happens, it goes into the dustbin (of history, or the spirit). An event will be retrieved only if it illustrates the correctness of the master's views or condemns the errors of the seditious. It is made into an example. As for meaning, it is fixed in doctrine (Orwell hated the doctrinaire). The guardian of meaning needs the sustenance of the event only when summoning it to appear at the proceedings instituted by doctrine against the real. Nothing must happen but what is announced, and everything that is announced must happen. The promise and its keeping amount to the same thing.

Let us recall — in opposition to this murder of the instant and singularity — those short pieces in Walter Benjamin's *One Way Street* and *A Berlin Childhood*, pieces Theodor Adorno would call "micrologies." They do not describe events from childhood; rather they capture the childhood of the event and inscribe what is uncapturable about it. And what makes an encounter with a word, odor, place, book, or face into an event is not its newness when compared to other "events." It is its very value as initiation. You only learn this later. It cut open a wound in the sensibility. You know this because it has since reopened and will reopen again, marking out the rhythm of a secret and perhaps unnoticed temporality. This wound ushered you into an unknown world, but without ever making it known to you. Such initiation initiates nothing, it just begins.

You fight against the cicatrization of the event, against its categorization as "childishness," to preserve initiation. This is the fight fought by writing against bureaucratic Newspeak. Newspeak has to tarnish the wonder that (something) is happening. The same thing is at stake for the guerrilla of love against the code of feelings: to save the instant from what is customary or understood.

And I should add — giving the "New-" in Newspeak its due, and recognizing that the real basis of totalitarianism (in 1984) is economic and mass mediatized rather than political — I should add, saving the instant from innovation, that other mode of the already said. Innovation is for selling. A sale anticipates the destruction of an object in its use or usury and, by acquitting the account, anticipates the end of a commercial relationship. When we are quits, nothing has happened; we quit. We can only re-commence. The trade in novelty leaves no trace, opens no wound — no more than any other trade.

I now come to the second aspect of 1984 illuminated by Claude Lefort: the body. Lefort is concerned with the looks, gestures, and attitudes that create a continuity between the reality recounted by Orwell, the past as Winston remembers it, and Winston's dreams. The hero's present relationships with O'Brien and Julia are thus interwoven with the life he led as a child and the image of his mother.

Lefort uses the name of the body to designate the two entities Merleau-Ponty tried to consider together in *The Visible and the Invisible:* the knot that ties the sentient to the sensible, the chiasm of sensibility, the phenomenological body; and the hidden, singular organization of space-time, the phantasm, the psychoanalytic body. The body that is joined to the world, of which it is a part, which it composes and which composes it; and the body that removes itself from the world into the darkness of what it has lost, there to come alive.

In each case we are concerned with an idiom, an absolutely singular, untranslatable way of deciphering what is happening. The point of view, the point of listening, of touch, of scent, any point at which the sensible assaults me is not transferable in space-time. We call this singularity of resonance "existence." In language it hinges on deictics: *I, this, now, there,* etc., are ways to signal it. Even so, this experience or existence can be shared in its intransitivity. *Your* point of listening, of contact [*tact*], etc., will never be mine. The blinding enigma of the world of existences is that in it singularities are present in the plural: they constantly come into contact with one another through these fragile antennae of sensibility, this commotion of ants.

And, in this contact, love is the exception. It demands the permeability and the surrender of my field of perspective to yours. Hence the never-ending search for a different idiom of sensibility, this vertigo where my idiom and yours falter, where they look for exchange, where they resist and discover each other. This is what nakedness declares — I mean the nakedness of the couple. In language, it is declared by lovers' prattle, by the search for a common yet intransmissible idiom born in the mouth-to-mouth of two bare voices.

The other line of the body traced by Orwell, and followed by Lefort, is the phantasm: the terror of the past marked and masked by its presence, inscribed before it is felt, the secret manipulator of affections. The phantasm traces the line of greatest weakness. Winston's is a morbid dread of rats. O'Brien detects this phantasm, and by staging it, breaks down Winston's resistance.

Weakness compared to what? By what measure of strength? The phantasm is the idiom that is spoken in the idiom I speak. It speaks more softly than I do. It means to say something I do not mean to, something I do not say. The phantasm is a peculiarity at once more familiar and more strange than my point of sensibility. It commands that point; it makes me blind and deaf to what is otherwise visible and audible, allergic to what is inoffensive; it makes me experience delight where the canons of culture prescribe horror or shame. So it is weakness compared to the norm, a breakdown in relation to communicability.

By following this double line of the body, by deepening it, the bureaucratic (or commercial) master can get the insurgents to "give" each other up to the police. That they love one another is all it takes. Together they embraced the initiatory value of the event; together they stumbled around in the labyrinth of sensibility, sensuality, and naked speech; they revealed to themselves and to each other the most voracious figures controlling them. By "giving" (what a word) the object of love up to Big Brother, the lover betrays not only what both of them are but also what they are not, what they lack, their failing. An admission of weakness is the most prized of denunciations. It supplies the master with information and the means for obtaining it. An act is inscribed positively in reality; a trace of it can always be kept on record. But the part of everyone that waits, hopes, and despairs — that can never be captured and registered. Therein lies the true crime that precedes any criminal act.

The unconscious must be confessed and declared. At confession, Satan speaks the language of God, Kamenev the language of Stalin. Both sides of the case can be put; the differend between idiom and norm amounts to no more than minor litigation. Whether the criminal pays or does not pay is beside the point. What matters is that integrity and uniqueness have been restored to the language of communication by his confession and public declaration, even if they are forced. Every admission reinforces Newspeak, since it implies and complies with the renunciation of the potentialities of language: the eradication of differends and the annulment of the event to which they are tied. There is no place for idiom in Newspeak, just as there is no place for writing in the press and the media. As Newspeak spreads, culture declines. "Basic language" is the language of surrender and forgetting.

This theme has become a cliché since the trials of the 1930s. Less familiar is the machinery of denial imagined by Orwell. This is because it works by love and writing, by what love and writing dare to uncover and what they alone can betray — unnameable singularity. Khruschev used to say that the GPU's secret for extracting confessions was simple: strike, strike, and strike again. Despotism as Orwell imagines it does not (only) torment need, it seduces desire. Whether it works like this in particular cases is debatable. But for Orwell at least, it is along this line of extreme weakness that resistance is put to the final test, along this line that the fate of a true republic is played out.

I mention the republic as a way of introducing one final thought for you. It is a commonplace to say that our situation in 1984 is not the one Orwell foresaw. But such a denial is too hasty. It is correct, at least for the West, as long as this situation is understood in a narrowly politicological or sociological sense. But when we consider the generalization of binary languages, the effacement of the difference between the here and now and the there and then that results from the spread of telerelations, the forgetting of feelings in favor of strategies (concomitant with the hegemony of commerce), we can see that the threats leveled at writing, love, and singularity, because of this situation, our situation, are essentially akin to the threats described by Orwell.

And like Claude Lefort, I think that if we dismiss Orwell's novel out of hand we repeat — obviously in a different register and a different genre, but repeat nonetheless — the action of the system's representative in his dismissal of Winston's testimony, his diary, and everything else. There is no question that a threat of a similar kind exists today, and this dismissal is one of its symptoms. What lends substance to this threat is, taken collectively or severally, the impact of mediatized democracies (the antithesis of the republic), technosciences working with and upon language, worldwide economic and military competition, and the general decline of "modern" ideals.

For at least two centuries modernity taught us to desire the extension of political freedoms, science, the arts, and technology. It taught us to legitimate this desire because, it said, this progress would emancipate humanity from despotism, ignorance, barbarism, and poverty. The republic is the humanity of citizens. Today this progress continues, assuming the more shameful name of development. But it is now impossible to legitimate development by promising emancipation for humanity as a whole. This promise has not been kept. It was broken, not because it was forgotten, but because development itself makes it impossible to keep. The new illiteracy, the impoverishment of people in the South and the Third World, unemployment, the tyranny of opinion and the prejudices then echoed in the media, the law that performance is the measure of the good — all this is due not to a lack of development, but to development itself. This is why we would no longer dream of calling it progress.

The promise of emancipation was rekindled, championed, and expounded by the great intellectual, that category born of the Enlightenment, defender of ideals and the republic. Intellectuals of today who have chosen to perpetuate this task in ways other than a minimal resistance to every totalitarianism, who have been imprudent enough to nominate the just cause in conflicts between ideas or powers — the likes of Chomsky, Negri, Sartre, Foucault — have been tragically deceived. The signs of the ideal are hazy. A war of liberation does not indicate that humanity is continuing to emancipate itself. Nor does the opening of new markets indicate humanity's increasing wealth. Schooling no longer delivers citizens; at best it delivers professionals. So what legitimation could we put forward for the pursuit of development?

Adorno understood the distress I am speaking about better than most of his successors. He associates it with the collapse of metaphysics, and particularly with the decline of an idea of politics. He turns to art, not in order to calm this no doubt irremissible distress, but to bear witness to it and, I would say, to save its honor. This is what Orwell's novel does.

I am not saying that the line of resistance traced by Orwell's work is not without problems. Quite the reverse. The appeal to modern ideals was an appeal to the universality of reason. Ideas are argued out and arguments lead to conviction. Reason is in principle universally shared. But we have seen that this is not strictly true of the body, and certainly not of the unconscious body (if I can call it that), which imprisons each one of us in an incommunicable secret.

This is why I feel we must extend the line of the body in the line of writing. The labor of writing is allied to the work of love, but it inscribes the trace of the initiatory event in language and thus offers to share it, if not as a sharing of knowledge, at least as a sharing of a sensibility that it can and should take as communal.

We have a number of negative signs that writing (or "art": as you know, different media, including the electronic media, can be used in writing) might be a line of resistance. We only have to remember the fate that political totalitarianisms set aside for the so-called historical "avant-gardes." Or observe, in the alleged "surpassing" of avant-gardism today — and on the pretext of returning to communication with the public — the disdain felt for the responsibility of resisting and bearing witness that, for at least a hundred years, was assumed by the avant-gardes.

The problems created by the resistance I am describing will continue to surface. It is for us to elaborate them, as it will be for you. What I want to say to you is simply this: following this line does not mean shutting ourselves away in ivory towers or turning our backs on the new forms of expression bestowed on us by contemporary science and technology. It means that we use these forms in an attempt to bear witness to what really matters: the childhood of an encounter, the welcome extended to the marvel that (something) is happening, the respect for the event. Do not forget that you were and are this yourself: the welcomed marvel, the respected event, the childhood shared by your parents.

Chapter 10

Address on the Subject of the
Course of Philosophy

To Hugo Vermeren
Nanterre, October 20, 1984

If I am to believe the prospectus for the "Education and Philosophy" seminars sent to me by your father, the issue for our reflection is the training [*formation*] of teachers in philosophy, assuming that "educating and instructing are philosophical acts." A few words to the son.

I'm not sure what "philosophical act" would mean. I am going to give a precise meaning to the word *act*, opposing it to potential. And I will say that philosophy is not an entity, a potential, a "body" of knowledge, knowledge of how things should be done or what to feel — but simply that it is in action. I have to confess to you that in my opinion educating and instructing are not any more or less "philosophical acts" than banqueting or fitting out a ship. Philosophy is not a discrete terrain in the geography of the disciplines. Everyone knows that.

I say "course of philosophy" as one says "thread of time." We know that a major part of philosophical reflection since Protagoras and Plato, since Pythagoras, has revolved around the word *training* (*Bildung*), and thus around pedagogy and *reform*. The assumption is that the mind is not given to human beings as it should be and has to be re-formed. Childhood is the monster of philosophers. It is also their accomplice. Childhood tells them that the mind is not given. But that it is possible.

Training means a master coming to the aid of the possible mind in childhood, while it is still awaiting self-fulfillment. You are familiar with the *circulus vitiosus:* but what about the master? How did he free himself from his childhood monstrosity? Educating the educators, reforming the reformers: you'll follow the aporia from Plato through Kant up to Marx. Should we say of training what is said of psychoanalysis? Just as there was a founding self-analysis, was there also a founding self-training? An autodidact, father of all didactics?

Philosophers differ from psychoanalysts in that they have many fathers, too many to accept just *one* paternity. Or alternatively, in that philosophizing is first and foremost an autodidactic activity.

That is the first thing I mean by course of philosophy. You cannot be a master and master this course. You cannot open up a question without leaving yourself open to it. You cannot scrutinize a "subject" (training, for example) without being scrutinized by it. You cannot do any of these things without renewing ties with the season of childhood, the season of the mind's possibilities.

You need to recommence. You cannot be a philosopher (not even the teacher of philosophy) if your mind is made

up on a question before you arrive, if in class it does not
commence, if it does not resume the course from the beginning. For a start, we all know that this work must take place
on the occasion of any question or "subject" at all. Second,
we know that commencing does not mean proceeding gene-
alogically (as if genealogy, and especially the diachrony of
historians, were not in question). The monster child is not
the father of the man; it is what, in the midst of man, throws
him off course [*son dé-cours*]; it is the possibility or risk of
being adrift. We always begin in the middle. This is why
the project of a degree course in philosophy, a project
transposed from the exact sciences, looks doomed to failure.

All the same, "autodidacticism" does not imply that you
can learn nothing from others. Only that you learn nothing
from them unless they themselves learn to unlearn. The
course of philosophy is not propagated in the way a body
of knowledge is transmitted. It is not done by acquisition.

This is clear in the case of philosophical reading, which
makes up a large part of the dialogue we have with ourselves
on a particular "subject." This reading is philosophical, not
because the texts being read are philosophical — they could
just as easily be by artists, scholars, or politicians. And you
can read texts without philosophizing. Reading is only philosophical when it is autodidactic, when it is an exercise in
discomposure in relation to the text, an exercise in patience.
The long course of philosophical reading is not just learning what has to be read, it is learning that reading is never
finished, that you can only commence, and that you have
not read what you have read. Reading is an exercise in
listening.

Forming in yourself this capacity for listening in reading
is forming yourself in reverse; it is losing your proper form.
It is reexamining what is presupposed or taken as read in
the text and in the reading of the text. The essential thing
about what we call elaboration — which both accompanies

and discloses patient listening — consists in this anamnesis, this inquiry into what remains as yet unthought, even when it is already thought. That is why philosophical elaboration bears no relation to theory, why the experience of this elaboration bears no relation to the acquisition of a specific knowledge (matheme), and why the resistance that one encounters in the work of listening and anamnesis is of a different order to the resistance that can impede the transmission of knowledge.

This course works on so-called reality: it strips away reality's criteria, it suspends reality itself. If gaining time is one of the principal criteria of reality and realism — and today this seems to be the case — then the course of philosophy does not conform to the reality of today. Our difficulties as teachers of philosophy are essentially bound up with the demand for patience. The idea that we could put up with not making progress (in a calculable and visible way), that we could put up with always doing no more than making a start — this is contrary to the general values of prospection, development, targeting, performance, speed, contracts, execution, fulfillment. I remember one thing that remained constant when I taught in secondary institutions: we, the students and I, were "at sea" throughout the first trimester. The course began, or rather began to begin, with the survivors in January. One had to — one has to — endure the childhood of thought. I realize that "conditions," as they say, are no longer the same. I will get back to this point.

I have nothing to teach you (by hypothesis). We all know that the philosophy course asks the same price as the course of philosophy. That is the price of conveying, by way of themes that may or may not be laid down in the program, examples of this work of recommencement drawn from the bibliography of philosophy, or signs of this same work taken from the history of science, technology, the arts, and politics.

So it is the price not only of making these examples and signs known, presenting them as the concerns or referents of scholarly discourse, but also, in a pragmatic sense, of inscribing the work of listening, anamnesis, and elaboration directly in class, inscribing it "live" in the small world of proper names where, for two hours, the stake of the day's class is put on the line. And the stake is always precisely that this work of thought should be taking place, following its course, in class, here and now.

This demand is not "pedagogical." It determines no method of teaching, no strategy for the teacher. Not even a style or a tone of teaching. There is nothing scientific about it. On the contrary: whenever the course of philosophy finds a place in the philosophy course, the result is that each class, each collection of names, dates, and places, elaborates an idiom, the idiolect in which this work is carried out. There is an affinity between the autodidact and the idiolect.

This singularity of the philosophy course — I mean, in this course and marking the course of this course — is the very singularity that marks the course of philosophy. I think writing a philosophical text, alone at one's desk (or taking a walk . . .), implies exactly the same paradox. We write before knowing what to say and how to say it, and in order to find out, if possible. Philosophical writing is ahead of where it is supposed to be. Like a child, it is premature and insubstantial. We recommence, but we cannot rely on it getting to the thought itself, there, at the end. For the thought is here, muddled up in the unthought, trying to make sense of the impertinent chatter of childhood.

At first glance, then, we see no essential difference between philosophizing and teaching philosophy. Kant says that one does not learn philosophy; at best one learns to philosophize (*philosophieren*). Whether alone or in the company of others, we are autodidacts — in the sense that the only way we learn how to philosophize is by philosophizing.

Now to my second point. Kant does, however, draw a distinction between the scholastic concept (*Schulbegriff*) of philosophy and its worldly concept (*Weltbegriff*). In the school, philosophizing is that exercise in patience that Kant, like Aristotle, calls dialectics. But when philosophy is cast into the world, Kant says it must assume an additional responsibility. Not only is it a test of what thinking is, it is also measured against an ideal, the ideal of the model philosopher who is the "legislator of human reason," as Kant writes. Philosophy in the world is charged with the task of referring knowledge, all kinds of knowledge, to the essential finalities of human reason. This is the demand that comes from the world — once philosophy is in the world, a practical and popular interest gets added to the speculative interest of reason (that work of endurance I spoke about earlier). As you know, and as Kant explains in the Dialectic of the first *Critique*, these interests are contradictory.

Does the teacher of philosophy today answer to the school or to the world? Modernity, the Enlightenment, and Kantian reflection itself placed the school at the center of the popular and practical interest of reason. For two centuries, above all in France and in a different way in Germany, the focus of this interest was called educating the citizen for the republic. The task of philosophy became confused with the task of emancipation. For Kant, emancipation is clearly the freedom left to reason in determining and accomplishing its ends, outside of any pathos. Such is the legislator of human reason.

This "modern" perspective contains the following assumption: the world asks philosophy to legislate practically and politically. It is not telling you anything new to say that we no longer ask whether it is right or wrong for the world to address this demand to the teacher of philosophy (in the world, via the school, for two centuries now). The question we ask is whether the world still addresses any demand of this sort to the teacher — or *any* demand, period.

If it is true that the philosophy course follows a philosophical course, if it is true that philosophizing, alone or in class, responds to a demand for a return to the childhood of thought, what would happen if thought no longer had a childhood? If those who pass for children or adolescents ceased to be the milieu of human uncertainty, the very possibility of ideas? If interests were already fixed? To my knowledge, secondary school teachers in France, in philosophy at least, do not need to be trained to philosophize. They are, which is to say that they never will be. That is how it should be. But they cannot deliver the course of philosophy they are capable of, simply because students are not given to patience, anamnesis, and recommencement.

I can see no pedagogical cure for this that would not be worse than the complaint. To instruct teachers to be indulgent, to advocate seduction or to prescribe demagogic overtures or gadgets for winning the children's favor is worse than the complaint. We have all had in our classes those Alcibiadeses who would come and tempt us in this way, but sooner or later we had to make them understand, like Socrates did with Alcibiades, that by wanting to trade off their seduction against our wisdom, which is worthless, they were buying into an exchange between dupes. The limit would be to advise philosophy teachers to turn each student into an Alcibiades. The work of anamnesis and elaboration actually happening in class, whether gay or serious, owes nothing to enticement.

This predicament is not unlike the one the Eleatic Stranger experiences in *The Sophist* (217c ff., 246c). One chooses to argue by question and answer when the other party has no problem about answering and is tractable, *euènios* (from *ènia*, the bit of the bridle). Otherwise it is better to argue alone. One can have a dialogue with the friends of forms; they are better domesticated than the "materialists" who reduce everything to the body. As far as the latter are concerned, the work of anamnesis is done in absentia, all alone, and on their behalf. One closes the school.

The decline of modern ideals, combined with the persistence of the republican institution of schooling that was sustained by these ideals, has the effect of plunging into the course of philosophy minds who never enter into it. Their resistance seems invincible precisely because it is without commitment. They speak the idiom "the world" has taught them, and still teaches them — and the world speaks of speed, satisfaction, narcissism, competitivity, success, and fulfillment. The speech of the world is ruled by economic exchange, generalized to every aspect of life, including affections and pleasures. Its idiom is totally different from the idiom of the course of philosophy — they are incommensurable. There is no judge to apportion this differend. The student and teacher are victims of one another. There can be no course of dialectics or dialogics between them; there can only be agonistics.

Three final remarks:

First, from what I have said here, my conclusion is not that teachers of philosophy need to be trained for war (the war of words, it goes without saying). But I do remember that the main reason invoked by Aristotle for the study of rhetoric and dialectics is that the one who is right at school can easily be defeated in the agora. Now, if I am not mistaken, the agora is in the school. I also recall that Kant portrays the philosopher (not the teacher, I admit) as a warrior ever vigilant, crossing swords with the merchants of transcendental appearance. We ought to be capable of confronting a mass of malevolent opinion. But we must also elaborate our resolve, and try to find out what good we are fighting for.

Next, there is the Platonic solution: select the minds capable of pursuing the course of philosophy. And the Pythagorean solution: separate the *mathématikoi* from the *politikoi*. Today this would mean breaking with democratism in favor of a republic of minds, and leaving it to others to look after the running of the demos. Philosophy becomes an optional subject: it is either dropped at later levels or taught only in certain secondary institutions. Everything is heading toward this sort of outcome, however things may stand at the moment. Here again, we need to elaborate an approach for thought and weigh up the stakes.

There is one final point that we must not ignore. The call for anamnesis, discomposure, and elaboration has not disappeared, although it may be in short supply. Above all, it is being deferred. What we see at Vincennes (University of Paris-VIII) is a listening public of men and women who, in their working lives, pursue the most varied professions. Again it is the agora, but here a benevolent one. The motive behind this call for philosophy is not so much the stifling nature of these jobs as the obscurity of their goals. The professions concerned all require qualifications, sometimes high qualifications: science, law, medicine, the arts, journalism. The level of the qualifications generally required for such work brings with it a certain avant-gardism, questions about the nature of the activity to be performed, a desire to rewrite the institution. In setting its course, philosophy (or the philosopher) should bear in mind that this questioning can occur at any time. This is what the Collège International de Philosophie, for example, tries to do. Maybe there is more childhood available to thought at thirty-five than at eighteen, and more outside a degree course than in one. A new task for didactic thought: to search out its childhood anywhere and everywhere, even outside childhood.

Afterword: Reading against Literacy

Wlad Godzich

Le Postmoderne expliqué aux enfants (*The Postmodern Explained* [to Children]) is a title, and a book, in need of explanation. Originally published in 1986 but written between 1982 and 1985, the letters that constitute the book are addressed to the children, and in some instances, infants, of Lyotard's friends and colleagues. They were written just after Lyotard had finished writing *Le Différend*, and they mark a return to the issues raised by *The Postmodern Condition* published in French in 1979 and the object of controversy ever since. The title of the book has suggested to some a prank and perhaps even some impatience with the tenor of the debate that has raged around the notion of the postmodern. It is dead earnest and nothing if not patient, however, as I shall try to show. One needs to read it in the context of the two earlier books, both published in English by the University of Minnesota Press, in order to understand the seriousness of the title and the patience of the book.

When Jean-François Lyotard published *Le Différend* in December 1983 he described it as "mon livre de philosophie" (my philosophical book), a denomination that was bound to raise more than one eyebrow. It suggested that all of his prior works, which numbered then some twelve books and a hundred articles, had not been philosophical but something else, at best perhaps a prolegomenon to his future philosophical book. This appellation was also a rather transparent allusion to Friedrich Nietzsche's *Philosophenbuch*, the unfinished book of what one is forced to call a miscellany (if only to hold the word "heterogeneity" in reserve) of aphorisms, sketches of arguments, and full-fledged essays including the justly famous "On Truth and Lie in the Extramoral Sense." Was Lyotard burying his earlier work with the suggestion of a posthumous work published, as the great Portuguese poet and modernist mystifier Fernando Pessoa put it, "pre-posthumously"? In an oeuvre already marked by sudden turns and discontinuities, was *Le Différend* to be the most radical turn of all? Or was Lyotard just being provocative and teasing?

That he could be provocative would surprise no one; he had been, after all, the wild man, albeit of the gentlest kind, of French philosophy for nearly twenty years, a name to be shunned in the circles of official academic philosophy whose hostility to Lyotard stemmed as much from his radical political past as from his writings. This political past needs to be evoked for the English-language reader who may not be familiar with French fringe politics. Lyotard had long been torn between the life of writing and the life of militant political action. He saw thinking and writing as an ascetic, if not monastic, activity, and was prepared to dedicate himself to it when his personal circumstances pushed him in the opposite direction. He was part of the original collective of the small but highly influential Socialisme ou Barbarie, an independent left-wing group that was responsible for, among other things, an analysis of the Soviet Union as bureaucratic totalitarianism. Lyotard taught philosophy in then French Algeria just prior to the outbreak of the war of national liberation, and he actively and publicly embraced the cause of the Algerians without regard for the risk this position entailed. This involvement did not represent an *engagement* on his part (and of his family) along the lines advocated by Sartre during those years, for nothing could be further removed from Lyotard than the concern with subjectivity evidenced by Sartre, a concern that was all too petit bourgeois as far as Lyotard was concerned. Nor is it clear that the politics of *engagement* were really open to him; they were meant, after all, for intellectuals in need of action, and it is far from certain that Lyotard thought of himself as an intellectual then. To be sure, 1954 was the year in which he had published his first book, but he remained committed to militant activity, and his siding with the Algerians was nothing more than the exercise of his sense of justice (incidentally, the most developed of his senses). Back in metropolitan France he continued his activities on behalf of Algerian freedom fighters and engaged in various organizing efforts of the French working class especially in those industries where it was becoming clear that the unions controlled by the Communist party were not addressing genuine workers' concerns. Even when he decided to follow an academic and scholarly career, he did not abandon his militant ways, as is evidenced by his actions in the storming of the administration building occupied by Dean Paul Ricoeur at Nanterre in May 1968, one of the major events of that fateful month and premonitory of much that was to follow.

This brief sketch of Lyotard's life up to the point where he is about to dedicate himself to writing may suggest that he is a late avatar of that abiding romantic myth: the man of action. Nothing could be further from the truth. Whereas in that myth action is elevated to redemptive status for the one who undertakes it, for Lyotard it becomes a source of interrogation: What presides over our actions? What is their end? Why do we act? In other words, the problem of agency is one of his central concerns, and he sees it as underlying the historical epoch we call modernity. Lyotard will devote much of his energy after 1968 to an understanding of the predicaments of modernity, first by exacerbating some of the modernist positions in *Discours, figure* and in the notorious *L'Economie libidinale* with its denunciations of theory and of the theoretical enterprise.

It was shortly after the publication of *L'Economie libidinale* in 1974 that Lyotard began working on *Le Différend*, a work that would take nine years to complete, though it should be said that these nine years were punctuated by the publication of some additional eight books, several monographic works on painting, and over sixty articles, including the famous *Postmodern Condition* of 1979, originally written as a commissioned report for the Université de Québec system. Indeed, the reader of *Le Différend* is constantly reminded of these works, not by the author but because she or he finds in *Le Différend* an explanation, or at least a foundation, for what was being asserted in more lapidary fashion in such works as *Instructions païennes* or even *The Postmodern Condition*. Since it is in these years that Lyotard became known as the theoretician of the postmodern — a title thrust on him and certainly not self-imposed — the question inevitably arises whether *Le Différend*, as his philosophical book, is a philosophy of the postmodern.

The question does not admit of a simple answer. There is, for instance, something postmodern about the organization of this philosophical book, such as the "Reader's Notice," which ostensibly precedes the text and describes succinctly all aspects of the book for those readers who wish to talk about it without having to bother reading it. This apparent playfulness is in dead earnest; it is a preemptive strike against all those who would be tempted to summarize or to paraphrase the book. If such is your wish, do not exert yourself, says the "Notice"; it is already done, here it is. If your way of dealing with books, with knowledge in general, is to consume it, here it is, prepackaged just for you. The "Reader's Notice," in other words, puts the reader on notice that what remains is to *read* the book, a mode of enactment of it that excludes summary or paraphrase. My remarks in these pages can do no more than suggest what a reading of *Le Différend* might entail, and in the process, enact it as a philosophy of the postmodern.

The "Reader's Notice," which one should probably render as the "Reader's Digest," connects *Le Différend* to the observation that Lyotard uses as his point of departure in *The Postmodern Condition*, namely, that the status of knowledge has deeply altered in postindustrial societies. Within such societies, knowledge is treated as the major force of production and is increasingly dissociated from the individuals who possess it in order to become a commodity in the marketplace; it is redefined in terms of specifiable bits of information, and its chief function is to ensure the optimal performance of the system. Positive knowledge is subjected to a process of commodification in which it is reduced to quanta of information that can be machine processed. For Lyotard, this altered status of knowledge is one of the major features of what he calls the postmodern condition. The other major characteristic is a consequence of the first: the objectification of knowledge — that is, its separation from human beings — brings about a new cultural environment in which there is marked loss of faith in what Lyotard called the metanarratives of legitimation. In *The Postmodern Condition* Lyotard approached both of these issues from a sociological perspective and attributed the process of the commodification of knowledge to a structural development of societies that find themselves increasingly forced to rely on machine-processable knowledge. He did not, however, seek an external cause (e.g., the rise of technoscience in advanced capitalism) for the disinclination felt toward the metanarratives of legitimation, but attempted instead to locate it in these metanarratives themselves by showing their inherent vulnerability, so that Lyotard's procedure amounted in effect to a delegitimation of the narratives of the legitimation of knowledge. This procedure has been the object of considerable misprision: whereas Lyotard was intent on showing the structural flaws of these metanarratives, he has been perceived as their cause. We should bear in mind that the issue of the legitimacy of knowledge is the underlying problem of modernity inasmuch as the latter cut itself off from divine guarantees of knowledge, so that the problem that haunts all modern thinkers from Descartes, Locke, and Kant onward, is that of ensuring the reliability of knowledge (i.e., its legitimacy) and of all forms of individual and collective action that rest on it. Lyotard's approach runs counter to that of most other contemporary thinkers concerned with this issue. To better appreciate the angle he gives to the problem, it may be useful to take a brief look at two other writers who have struggled with this problem: Karl-Otto Apel and Jürgen Habermas.

Apel goes right to the heart of the problem: the realm of science and that of ethics have gone their separate ways; as a result human actions are no longer grounded in theoretical knowledge, and theoretical knowledge is, for its part, unable to legitimate itself. How did this separation come about? Through the disappearance of a transcendental subject capable of mediating between the realms of the scientific and of the ethical. The most urgent task is therefore that of reconstructing this transcendental subject. Apel does not indicate what brought about the demise of the transcendental subject erected by Kant in his canonical organization of the mind's faculties, but his solution does suggest that it is the fact that Kant's philosophy gave rise to two distinct traditions, the analytic and the synthetic, and that the task at hand consists therefore in reuniting them. It is not surprising then to see him attempt a large synthesis of the German philosophical tradition, principally phenomenology and hermeneutics, with the linguistic analysis practiced by Anglo-American philosophy as a way of reestablishing the transcendental conditions of reliable knowledge. (I use the term *transcendental* here in its Kantian sense as indicating the conditions of the possibility of reliable knowledge.)

This requires him to establish first the fact that the findings of science are predicated on a measure of intersubjective validity, and then to raise the question of the subject in science at large as a way of bringing forth the transcendental subject he seeks to reconstruct. The stakes should be clear: Apel sees a disjunction between science as the realm of reliable cognition, and ethics as the domain of praxis. The problem is twofold: praxis (i.e., human action, individual as well as collective) will be arbitrary and anarchic, ruled by self-interest, passions, and ideology, if it cannot be anchored in reliable knowledge of the real, but the reliability of knowledge is very much in question as knowledge becomes a commodity like any other. Hence the need for a salvage operation. And since what is at stake is the very economy of knowledge and praxis in modernity, it is modernity itself that Apel seeks to save.

The course of this salvage operation, indeed the road to salvation, must follow the linguistic turn of twentieth-century philosophy as far as Apel is concerned. In this way, the problem of the intersubjective validation of science is displaced from the plane of individual consciousnesses of the knowing subjects and their communion to that of language itself, and since the problem entails issues of language in use, it is the pragmatic dimension of language that will be seen as most promising of resolution. By the same token it allows Apel to invoke the work of the American semiotician and pragmatist Charles Sanders Peirce in preference to the canonical Kant. It will be recalled that for Kant the objective validity of knowledge was the result of the synthesizing activity of consciousness, and the latter was described in the *Critique of Pure Reason* as a system of faculties. Peirce, on the other hand, is far more reluctant to embrace the Kantian Rube Goldberg-type construction of the human mind, and he grounds the validity of knowledge in the semantic consistency of a representation arrived at by the interpretation of signs. Apel seizes on this dimension of sign interpretation, for he sees it as the potential unifier among all the sciences. The unity of intersubjective interpretation is no longer the property of an individual consciousness and is thus not subject to its vagaries, but resides within the continuity of the process of semiosis itself. It necessarily implies the idea of a community of interpretation that is both boundless and capable of increasing knowledge. Apel focuses on Peirce's "indefinite community of investigators" and elevates it to a quasi-transcendental status, for it is at this level that he believes a passage can be built between the realms of science and of ethics. Peirce had argued that the pragmatic conception of the process of knowledge formation necessarily required the positing of a community dedicated to the furtherance of knowledge.

He called this community a form of "logical socialism" by way of marking his distance from the Kantian approach to knowledge, which was grounded entirely in the individual and postponed the intersubjective validation to considerations of *sensus communis* and consensus — a problem Kant "solved" most unsatisfactorily by eradicating differences between subjects: consensus is inevitable if all those called on to consent are mutually interchangeable. Apel follows Peirce's lead and shows that a knowing subject engaged in a quest for knowledge must surrender his or her private interests in the name of a community yet to come, and she or he must do so on equally compelling logical (or theoretic) and moral (or ethical) grounds. In terms of linguistic pragmatics this implies that an individual who engages in an argument identifies with the rational norms that govern arguments of this type within this community (bearing in mind that this community, which is empirically determinable, must be boundless or infinite in principle — open-ended as we would say). It further implies, but on the social plane this time, that such a subject must be animated by the will to actually and effectively bring about the existence of such a community. And such a community can take the place of the Kantian subject, for it does more than this subject did: it does not merely synthesize knowledge, it *provides meaning*. Meaning is indeed the key here that Apel has sought in Peirce: unlike the synthesis effected by Kant's Understanding (*Verstand*), which remains caught within the boundaries of an individual consciousness, it opens up into a communicative comprehension that includes an ethical dimension.

Apel can now turn to this ethical dimension and provide the foundations of a reflective and critical practice of social sciences that would be free of the problems inherent in their prevailing positivistic model. Here he reactivates part of the well-established German hermeneutical tradition and its criticism of positivistic social sciences. First he accuses them of having uncritically imported into social science (*Geisteswissenschaften*) the subject/object split found in the natural sciences (*Naturwissenschaften*); second, he takes them to task for having far too reductive a concept of experience. As a result positivist social sciences embrace social behaviorism, track empirical regularities, and conceive of causality in human affairs as determined by behavior. Apel's alternative is a social science that conceives of society as the subject of historical experience, and this experience is in fact a historical self-experience of society, so that causal modes of explanation are discarded in favor of a reflective interpretation. Such an interpretation may start with a description of observable behavior in the source of the performance of an action, but it must go on to an evaluation of the ends of this action. And any evaluation, Apel is quick to remind us, must appeal to some norms, in this instance to the rational norms that prevailed before the action was undertaken. In other words, Apel's alternate form of social science must take the form of a hermeneutic reconstruction of historical experience, a reconstruction that must take place within the necessary context of his quasi-transcendental interpretive community of unlimited communication, which we can now see as a normative reference for his critique of existing institutions.

And yet Apel finds himself stymied at this point: he still cannot ground his understanding of human agency. He turns to Wittgenstein in order to do so, and more specifically to his notion of language game, which he interprets in a highly personal way. Since a language game is a set of rules by which some use of language is governed, Apel takes it that the language game provides the a priori structure of meaning available in any action situation in which it will be played. In other words, he treats the language game as an ideal type, and he connects it to his earlier pragmatic considerations of meaning. As a result he can develop the notion of a "transcendental language game" that is supposed to solve the vexing problem left over from Wittgenstein of how various empirical language games connect with one another: the transcendental language game provides an a priori communicational connection between any and all of them. Apel concedes that such a language game has to be a postulate of his theory, but this concession is made to mask the fact that the postulate in fact begs the very question it purportedly answers, namely, to account for the unity of the community of interpretation. In point of fact, Apel cannot ground this community except by making an unwarranted appeal to the dues ex machina notion of a transcendental language game. Richard Rorty, whose approach to these issues is not all that different from Apel's, refuses this type of solution and prefers to appeal to what he calls the conversational rules of existing interpreting communities, which amounts to giving normative status to the empirical, a gesture that is consonant with Peircian pragmatism but one that leaves him incapable of mounting a critique of existing conditions — something that Apel at least attempts — since one can validate one's discourse only by existing norms.

I have described Apel's attempt to extricate us from the predicament of modernity at some length because it reconnoiters quite well the range of available options for dealing with this predicament. We will see that Lyotard traverses some of the same terrain, but before returning to him, I want to turn briefly to one of his severest critics, Jürgen Habermas and *his* solution to the problem.

Habermas began by pursuing the Frankfurt school project of a critique of positivism, but we will see that his critique will eventually bring him around to espouse positions that his predecessors in the Frankfurt school had attacked earlier. His own alternate program takes the form of a theory of communicational activity, which he sees as grounded in a materialist social anthropology, despite its transcendental dimension. His anthropological doctrine is articulated around a dichotomy pitting the concept of "work" against that of "interaction," and this dichotomy in turn governs the crucial distinction between "instrumental activity" and "communicational activity." Habermas also returns explicitly to Kant's foundational distinction between pure and practical reason, recasting them as cognitive or theoretic uses of reason versus moral, practical ones. He also invokes the Kantian notion of an interest of reason to argue that there is always to be found a practical commitment of reason in favor of the rational itself, and that such a commitment implies, at the social level, the existence of a will toward social and political emancipation.

The reader will not have failed to observe that in spite of a different point of departure, Habermas elaborates a conceptual structure that will enable him to do what Apel was trying to accomplish, namely, to ensure the reliability of knowledge, to validate the critique of existing institutions and actions, and to ground human agency. Indeed, with his conceptual framework, Habermas can extend the Frankfurt school critique of modern rationality, which, it will be recalled, was accused by Adorno and Horkheimer of reifying Western rationality in favor of a strictly instrumental rationality within the framework of late capitalism. Habermas, however, seeks to safeguard a concept of rationality — which he will ground in the notion of communicational action — in order to arrive at normative criteria for the critique of society and to manage to escape from the complete instrumentalization of reason.

The instrumentalization of reason rests on the expulsion of the human subject from the cognitive loop by limiting knowledge to those forms of it that are subsumed by a theory of adequation to reality. Ideologically such an epistemological amputation leads to the expectation that only scientific and technological solutions are "serious" solutions to the problems faced by individuals and by society. At the level of practical reason, freedom of choice is restricted to options between technical variables. Human agency is thus neutralized, and the social subject of history is reified. At the same time prevalent forms of domination are legitimated since the only choices left are options of their own design. Habermas's solution is easy to guess: at the epistemological level he calls for a reinsertion of the scientific practices into their own contexts in order to bring out the falsehood of their claim to being determined by purely rational considerations; at the political level, he views the reclaiming of the public sphere from increasingly encroaching reification as the most urgent task. This solution requires the reintroduction of a normative framework that, according to Habermas, had been eliminated by positivism.

This normative framework will be articulated by the opposition of "work" and "interaction," which is meant to delimit precisely the realm of technical activity from that of practical reason, and thereby restore the importance of the sphere of interaction mediated by language. "Work" refers to a material practice intent on a mastery of nature by means of all available technical knowledge. "Interaction," on the other hand, refers to a symbolic social practice oriented toward an ethical and political objective: the emancipation of the social subject that takes place through the liberation of communicational activity.

When we engage in work we posit a goal for ourselves, we want to produce something as efficiently as we can. We rely on technical know-how derived from prior experience; we go about it in a rational way, for work is a rational activity governed by its ends. Communicational activity, which Habermas defines as "interaction mediated by symbols," is not the polar opposite of work; on the contrary, it is articulated with it according to a hierarchy specific to a given society. It is only in contemporary late-capitalist society that this hierarchical articulation has been broken and that the subsystems of technical activity have become autonomous in relation to the world of interaction. Since this realm of interaction is itself governed by norms that define the behavior expectations of the subjects that live in it, the autonomy of the technical subsystems is tantamount to their separation from the cultural norms prevalent in the society and their constitution into a separate "culture" of their own, independent of human beings but with considerable power over them. In this way, the technical tends to absorb the institutional framework of our experiential world by imposing its form of rationality on them.

Habermas's alternative consists in mounting a defense of this institutional framework — indeed, in restoring its normative importance and thus securing the conditions necessary for the formation of the political will of the collective subject. Once restored, the institutional framework will provide the space within which the mediation between technical knowledge and ability on the one hand and the practical will of the society on the other can be elaborated in a far-reaching debate over the principles and norms that should govern practical action. His immediate goal is thus communication free of any constraint and acknowledged as normative, and the task at hand is to identify regulatory instances of this type of communication. This leads Habermas to explore a universal pragmatics based on the normative concept of an ideal communicational situation, for it is this concept that defines the a priori conditions for the type of rational discussion that should prevail within situations of public deliberation (or practical discourse as Habermas likes to call it). This concept also has a critical function since it provides the norm by means of which one can diagnose distorted forms of communication, and especially the false consensus that obtains so frequently under present conditions. Habermas believes that this concept endows him with a quasi-scientific methodology, and he does not hesitate to describe its mode of application as proceeding by counterfactual demonstration: facts to be evaluated are measured by their relation to the norm the methodology enunciates.

As we have seen, Habermas starts out with a set of premises far removed from Apel's but he ends up with a pragmatic model of transcendental type nonetheless. And like Apel he locates the normative dimension of action at the level of a communicational understanding that opens unto the ethical dimension. In Apel the passage to the ethical was effected by generalizing Peirce's notion of a community of investigators into that of an ideal and normative community of unlimited communication; in Habermas the passage from the scientific (theoretic) to the ethical is effected in a more complex and critical way. Instead of the continuity implicit in Apel's generalization, we have a separation, if not an opposition, between two differing rationalities: a cognitive-technical one and an ethical-political one. In this Habermas is more faithful to Kant than Apel is: he maintains the differentiation of reason; he wants to rebuild its hierarchical articulation; and he insists on granting primacy to practical reason. In other words, he remains within the orbit of modernity.

We can now return to the Lyotard of *The Postmodern Condition*. We have seen that he has recast the opposition between the cognitive and the practical in terms of legitimation and that he too has adopted a pragmatic approach. But his reliance on the pragmatic does not lead in the direction of the ethical or the political, but rather serves to displace the focus of attention from the philosophical problem of legitimacy to the more methodological question of legitimation. This move toward an almost technical use of pragmatics allows Lyotard to avoid the troublesome area of normativity, which requires, as we have just seen in Apel and in Habermas, a search for criteria of legitimacy and inevitably leads to programs for salvaging modernity; he can concentrate instead on the analysis of actual legitimation procedures. Lyotard takes the two best-known accounts of the legitimation of knowledge — namely, the speculative narrative of German Idealism and the narrative of political emancipation of the Enlightenment — and shows first that they invoke different principles of legitimacy and that neither is capable of providing a full account of legitimation. Furthermore, Lyotard shows that each of these narratives must control a number of differing language games and must articulate them in a particular fashion; yet neither of these two master narratives has the capability to formulate the language game that can control and articulate their embedded language games. The result is a progressive erosion and eventual disintegration of the master narratives, a process we experience as loss of legitimation.

Lyotard's own alternative consists in taking the multiplicity of these heterogeneous language games as the basis for a pluralistic social pragmatics that he derives from the actual practices of scientific research. This is what he calls the postmodern, and this is where he separates himself from Apel and Habermas irrevocably, for he abandons the former's attachment to underlying stable systems and the latter's search for consensus. Legitimation, as practiced by researchers in mathematics and microphysics, relies not on the continuous exploitation of a proven paradigm but on the properly imaginative capacity of coming up with new and unheard of rules. Moreover, this search for new rules cannot proceed by consensus, since it must break with whatever paradigm is prevalent. Its operative principle is thus *dissensus*, which Lyotard will come to call *le différend*. It will be noted, however, that Lyotard's solution remained internal to the state of society described and analyzed. Unlike Apel and Habermas, Lyotard in *The Postmodern Condition*, did not propose any alternative to the system as a whole — something that he could not legitimately do given his focus on methodological issues. Habermas, apparently blind to the formal requirements of Lyotard's argument, latched on to this feature to call him a neoconservative.

Lyotard makes a first attempt to come to terms with this charge in *Au Juste*, a set of conversations recorded over seven days; I translated this under the title *Just Gaming*, which I hoped would prove as polysemic as the original, though in a displaced way. Just as in *The Postmodern Condition* he had juxtaposed the two canonical master narratives of modernity in order to deconstruct them, in this work Lyotard subjects to scrutiny two major accounts of justice: (1) the Platonic or ontological model in which the practice of justice is legitimate if it is derived from a prior theoretic discourse in which the very essence of justice is formulated; (2) the modern or Enlightenment model in which the practice of justice is just (i.e., legitimate) if it enforces laws that an autonomous collective subject has legislated for itself.

As far as the ontological, or Platonic, theory of justice is concerned, Lyotard shows, in a deft admixture of Kant and Wittgenstein, that a prescriptive discourse cannot be derived from a descriptive one: from an *is* one cannot derive an *ought*. It is a logical falsehood to pretend that the true and

the just are not dissociated. Furthermore, prescriptive statements not only cannot be derived from descriptive or deno-
tative ones, but in fact they cannot be grounded; they must
be precariously self-standing. We are then in what Lyotard
calls ''paganism,'' a state of affairs in which the practice
of justice must take place without reference to models.

As far as the modern theory is concerned, Lyotard chal-
lenges the idea of the autonomy of the subject as enunciator
of the law by showing that such an act of enunciation always
presupposes a chain of prior enunciations and enunciators,
none of which can claim originary status except as a character in a mythic discourse that needs to be enunciated in
any case. His reference here is also to pagan symbolic economy, but this time it is the narrative practices of primitive
societies that he invokes in order to show that the narrator
of a story defines himself (the example he adduces has only
male narrators) not as the first author of the story but as
a relay in a narrative of which he has been the recipient.
Lyotard insists on this detail because he wants to bring out
the fact that the active pole in this sort of discourse is that
of the narratee and not that of the narrator. And this fact
needs to be brought out because it is a constitutive feature
of modernity to actively forget it (i.e., to repress it) as it
presents itself under the guise of the epic of enunciative
autonomy, more commonly known as the advent of the freestanding individual subject. Lyotard can thus pursue his
further characterization of the postmodern by opposing
pagan heteronomy to the modern claim of autonomy.

Just Gaming grants absolute primacy to language games
and to their incommensurability. Lyotard is insistent, however, on a feature of language games that the Anglo-American tradition has not been particularly attentive to, namely,
the fact that one cannot logically derive a subject independ-
ently of a language game. In the Anglo-American tradition,

language games tend to be thought of as regulated forms of language use, and therefore presuppose the prior existence of a user. For Lyotard this is an unwarranted assumption since the assertion of the existence of such a user is specific to a language game itself that cannot have any incidence on other games given the incommensurability of games among themselves. It is the games that turn us into their players and not we who constitute games. Players are immanent to the games they play; as a result they cannot extricate themselves from these games and cannot produce a metadiscourse that could dominate this plurality. The only option that remains is that of an indefinite experimenting with language games, somewhat on the order of the scientific inventiveness that operates by rupture rather than continuous derivation. Such an experimenting Lyotard calls ''general literature.'' He recognizes, however, that this is more an account of our predicament in relation to the question of justice than a solution to it, and that he may be suspected of embracing a form of conventionalism. But in what language game could the solution be formulated? The only thing that can be done is to appeal to the Kantian notion of an Idea of Reason that will serve as the regulatory mechanism that will ensure that the incommensurability of language games is preserved, for ultimately, in *Just Gaming*, justice comes to be understood as being charged with the preservation of the purity of each language game and the prevention of the subservience of one language game to another.

Let us summarize things so far. Modernity, which Lyotard repeatedly equates with the unleashing of capitalism, presents human beings with a particular predicament with reference to their mode of being in the world and in relation to each other. Prior to modernity the relation they had to the world was taken to be one of knowledge, and this knowledge, on which individual and collective identities depended, was guaranteed by some divine instance or by some constitutive homology between humans and the world. Such a knowledge permitted humans to act, to build a world of human relations that increased the sum of knowledge — that is, their set of relations, their mode of being in the world. With the advent of modernity a change begins to take place in this economy: the old guarantees of knowledge cease to hold true and we are threatened with individual meaninglessness and collective tyranny, the latter understood as the arbitrary exercise of power. As if this were not worrisome enough, now knowledge is becoming autonomous from us and instead of anchoring us in the world, of ensuring the stability of our being in the world, begins to put us through its paces so that we do not know whether we are complying with a dynamic that is inherent and internal to its current level of development or whether we are being manipulated by some occult forces that control it. Several strategies of resistance are being mounted, mostly falling into two major types: those that seek to stabilize knowledge by anchoring it in some transcendental instance (Apel) and those that seek to protect or even reconquer the sphere of human action (Habermas, but this can also take the form of hope for the victory of margins believed to be somehow ''irreducible'' to the hegemonic process — the old Marcusian dream or the more recent Jamesonian vesting of historical hope in the Third World). There would be many who would view the linguistic turn in much recent thinking as an exacerbation of the erosion of human will and a subjection of human beings to a form of knowledge that is beyond our control. They would claim that we had gone too far. On the contrary, not far enough, Lyotard answers in *Le Différend*, and this is what makes that book so radical, and indeed a philosophy of the postmodern.

A philosophy of the postmodern must have a grounding different from that of the philosophy of modernity. It will be recalled that the very idea of such a grounding originates with Aristotle, who calls it *hypokeimenon*, that which, literally, underlies everything and thus allows everything else to stand. It will be further recalled that modernity is inaugurated philosophically with Descartes casting his methodic doubt upon this *hypokeimenon* and finding that it offers no ground for epistemological certainty, and that such a certainty can only be grounded in the thinking subject, the *cogito*, so that modernity can indeed be referred to as the epoch of the grounding subject. A postmodern philosophy needs to retrace this ground and pronounce itself on the matter of grounding, and Lyotard obliges by doing Descartes one better.

What resists Cartesian radical doubt is not the "Cogito," not the instance that says "I think," but the phrase "Dubito" (I doubt) — not the instance that says, "I doubt," for that would be the same Cartesian subject of enunciation, but the very phrase "Dubito," which is simply there, which happened and against which radical doubt bumps without being able to make it melt into air and is thus left with no other option than to proceed linking other phrases to it such as, "cogito, ergo sum." In other words, in a move that is as modern as they come, to the point of parodying this very procedure of foundationalism, Lyotard dislodges the anchor of modernity. Descartes believed that he had established the subject of the utterance as the ultimate guarantor of the statement; Lyotard establishes that such a statement has taken place and then proceeds to reverse the Cartesian chain of inferences using the Nietzschean model of reverse causality. It will be recalled that Nietzsche denounces the so-called naturalness of causality in the case of the bee sting, according to which first a bee stings us, then we feel pain, and we feel this pain as being caused by the bee. Nietzsche argues to the contrary that first we feel the pain, then we look for what may have happened to us; we see the bee, and we infer that the bee stung us, causing the pain, so that, for Nietzsche, the actual temporal sequence is not bee — sting — pain, but pain — bee — causal inference leading to the narrative of bee — sting — pain. Lyotard follows this model in his version of radical doubt and he obtains the following: first the phrase "Dubito," then the observation "I spoke," then the inference that there is an "I" that did the speaking and that it did so by virtue of a prior mental act of thinking, leading to the minimal canonical narrative of modernity: "Cogito, ergo sum." In Lyotard's retracing of Cartesian radical doubt, the "I," the subject, is an inference derived from the phrase "Dubito," which comes first and alone; it is an inference of the same order as Nietzsche's natural causality; that is, it is an inference authorized by the mode of functioning of the phrase "Dubito" *qua* phrase.

At first sight (but remember that *reading* is one of the stakes of the book), this may be taken as no more than an example of poststructuralist obstinacy; language before subjects; death of the author; end of humanism; and so on. But Lyotard's career shows that he is not an obstinate man though certainly a determined one. His determination in *Le Différend* becomes clearer when one notices that he drops all reference to language games because the notion of game still lends itself to anthropological appropriation, that is, to the idea that first there are subjects endowed with the capacity to decide to play language games. Lyotard will continue to search for a pragmatics but not an anthropological one, and that is the nature of his *différend* with Habermas and with Apel.

The term he uses instead of language game is *phrase*, which in French means sentence as well as phrase. Lyotard had used the term earlier, notably in relation to Auschwitz as the event that forces the reexamination of modernity. This term merits some attention, especially because of its occurrence in a book that retraces so much of the historical background of its emergence.

"Phrase" comes from the Greek *phrázein/phrazesthai:* to draw attention to, to watch for. This verb denotes an act of communication but one that does not involve sound or voice. It is never a synonym of *eipein,* which means to speak, in Homer, or of *légein,* which means to say, in post-Homeric Greek. *Phrázein* is related to *phrén* (thought, as in phrenology) as silent mental activity. Its synonyms are *semainen,* to signify, and *dèloûn,* to show. *Phrázein* designates the act of conveying a message by means of silent signs — gestures, for example. It refers to writing considered from the point of view of reading.

For the Greeks who lived the onset of literacy, writing did not speak, it did not encrypt a voice; it signified, indicated, showed. Theoretical discourse has been properly concerned with writing and its relation to voice, but it has been less attentive to reading. We need to remind ourselves of what the Greek experience of reading must have been at the very beginnings of literacy. To begin with, all reading was done aloud. There were technical reasons for this: the writing was a string of letters without breaks between words (the very idea of word existed but murkily), but the primary reason was because silent forms of speech did not exist. A sixth- or seventh-century B.C. Greek who comes upon an inscription (a phrase), most likely cut into the stone of a funerary monument, will begin to voice the letters. Most such monuments had inscriptions that read something like: "I am the repository of the glory of so-and-so." Our reader does not repeat words that were said by someone (the person whose body lies in the tomb never uttered them, and the monument never spoke), but he lends his voice, or she lends her voice, to these inscribed words. He lets his voice be occupied, appropriated, not by the words of another, but by words that were already there, without belonging to anyone. This is an important moment, for the intrusion experienced by the reader precipitates a sudden awareness of the self as this self is in fact invaded. It is not irrelevant to recall that some very early Greek inscriptions equate the process of reading with anal penetration. The sense of self is constituted in such a moment, and then the familiar process of natural causality takes over to induce the belief that such a self must have always already existed. Natural causality suppresses the importance of the moment of the constitution of the subject by leading to the inference that there had to have been such a subject all along for it to experience itself as invaded. But something of the originary experience persists in the term *egó,* whose etymology is that of "hereness," in other words, a pure deixis in time and space — indeed, the very ability to synthesize data (that is, the given) in space and time; the self as the subject of experience. The Greek reader is the deixis of the phrase as he or she is captured by it.

In an oral culture all of the foundational myths, stories, and their discourses reside outside of the individual in a vast *memoria* that is activated in performance. One never encounters this *memoria* except as another's voice outside or within oneself. In reading, something different happens: one lends one's voice to an element of *memoria;* one is dispossessed of one's own voice by something that does not have a voice in order that it may enter in relation with us by means of our own voice. The writing is certainly subjectless, but so are we before we read, since all subjecthood resides in the *memoria* as such (and not in its fragments). When the writing appropriates our voice in the act of reading it actually constitutes us as subjects, for reading enacts our relation to something that is outside us. And such subjects are not always already there; they are constituted in time and space, that is, in history.

We have seen that today it is knowledge itself that is becoming autonomous from us; yet it is in relation to this knowledge as the ultimate productive force of capitalism that we are being constituted as subjects, and not robbed of subjecthood or subjectivity as the modernistic account would have it. What troubles us is that we cannot have a relation of knowledge (a subject/object relation) to it for that would mean our subjugation, our objectification, and then we would have to take refuge in such strategies of weakness as seduction. Lyotard suggests that there is another type of relation that is open to us: those to be found in reading, all of them. For we must understand that reading is not actualizing something that lies there; it is deictically to anchor ourselves in relation to that which is around us, and such a deictic anchoring requires that to the phrase we voice we counterpose another phrase, that is, that we become the link in the concatenation of these phrases, with all this implies in terms of selection, organization, and ruse. It is not the transcendental positions of meaning that matter; it is how we deictically anchor such meaning as obtains around us. A postmodern philosophy is a political pragmatics of meaning.

Writing does not represent a voice; it is not even the image of a voice; it only aims to produce, to elicit, a voice that would result in an unresolvable dissensus, for this voice would mimetically imitate something that had never been in the order of voice. This dissensus, Lyotard's *différend*, is the condition of justice in a reading society, for it makes us into the kind of heteronomous pagan subjects that *Just Gaming* theorized. Such subjects are capable of the kind of justice that Eric Havelock recognized as existing among

these early Greeks, namely *dikè,* which is something that
cries aloud, in opposition to the much later *dikaiosúnè,* the
interiorized sense of justice that appears contemporaneously
with Socrates' logocentrism. It is the justice of heteronomy,
of irreducible difference. It is a type of justice whose exercise does not subject anyone to a law that is alien to him
or her and thus is not an injustice; it is a justice that does
not legislate and does not derive from legislation, but we
will see that it is not therefore lawless.

To close with the matter of reading, let us observe that
when an early Greek reader encounters *grammata* (silent
written signs), she or he is under the obligation of adding
(*epi*) some logos, as the Ionian word for reading (*épilégesthai*)
makes clear. In *Le Différend* Lyotard gives a text to read, a
text that invites us to *epi-logue* on modernity, to recognize
that the central problem of postmodernity is indeed that of
our ability to read, the problem of literacy, not in E. D.
Hirsch, Jr.'s sense or that of the advocates of so-called func-
tional literacy, but in the subject-constituting sense that
Lyotard develops in *Le Différend* and extends in the present
book.

It is now easier to see the seriousness behind the conceit
of the title: if reading is the mode of our constitution as subject, then we must return to this constitutive moment to
understand who we are and how we have come to be, how
we have effected the passage from being without language
(*in-fans,* the etymology of *enfant,* child) to wielders of language. There are two moments of great importance here
to Lyotard. The first is precisely that of this advent to language, this constitution of the subject in the act of reading,
for it yields the structure of the postmodern: only the modern believes that the subject comes first, fully constituted
to the act of reading. The actual sequence is that a child (of
whatever age, as the last essay makes clear) — that is, the

opposite of an autonomous subject — comes to the reading and is constituted by it in such a way that the belief in a prior subject is induced. This is the *post* of the modern, which always comes before the modern. The present book, which has the form of a series of letters to children, seeks to enact this moment of constitution in relation to a number of important themes that delimit the postmodern. But the foremost of these is that of reading, for it sets into motion the other themes without, however, acting as either their ground or their originator. Reading is an activity that must be ever renewed and is ultimately autodidactic.

And that is the second moment: the current concern with literacy is anchored in a conception of reading that is at a far remove from the kind of reading that Lyotard is concerned with. It is a view of reading that is modern in the extreme: it assumes the existence of a freestanding subject who must be equipped with the know-how to engage in a suitable technology of knowledge appropriation so that he or she may acquire knowledge, use it, transform it, and then exchange it. It is a literacy in the service of an apparatus of knowledge that is nothing more than Hegel's posthistorical state of Absolute Knowledge, that is, a series of articulated knowledge practices animated by the belief that nothing can escape their determination to arrive at a solution to any problem that may be posed to them. Children who are taught this sort of literacy become the servants of this knowledge apparatus. They are constituted by it as subjects to be sure, but in the sense of being subjected to it. Lyotard's notion of reading eschews such practicalities; it advocates a relentless relearning of reading, a reiteration of this constitutive moment, and a patience in its quest. Patience is a quality of children; impatience haunts teenagers, these beings who have been seduced out of childhood by the promises of a grown-up world that offers only its blandishments to them while preparing its ambush. Against such impatient reading, or the arrogant reading of the expert who is in "full possession" of the subject, Lyotard has invited us in these pages to once again learn how to read.

Index

Compiled by Hassan Melehy

Jean-François Lyotard is council member at the Collège International de Philosophie, professor emeritus at the University of Paris, and professor of French and Italian at the University of California at Irvine. The University of Minnesota Press has published his *Postmodern Condition: A Report on Knowledge* (1984), *The Differend: Phrases in Dispute* (1988), and *Heidegger and "the jews"* (1990). A collection titled *Political Writings* is forthcoming from Minnesota.

Wlad Godzich is professor of emergent literatures at the University of Geneva and the coeditor, with Jochen Schulte-Sasse, of the Theory and History of Literature series of the University of Minnesota Press.

Don Barry is a doctoral student in philosophy at the University of Sydney. He has published essays in philosophy and critical theory, as well as works of translation. He is an editor of *Local Consumption Publications.*

Bernadette Maher is a free-lance linguist, translator, and educational consultant working in the fields of language and literary theory.

Julian Pefanis is a lecturer at the Power Institute of Fine Arts at the University of Sydney, Australia. He is the author of *Heterology and the Postmodern* (1991), and has coedited and cotranslated a volume of essays by Jean Baudrillard, as well as other essays by Lyotard and Pierre Clastres.

Virginia Spate is the director of the Power Institute at the University of Sydney.

Morgan Thomas is a graduate student at the Power Institute and a free-lance writer.